Preschool Language
Manual

The Slow Learner Series
edited by Newell C. Kephart, Ph.D.

Preschool Language Manual

Irla Lee Zimmerman
Violette G. Steiner
Roberta L. Evatt

Charles E. Merrill Publishing Co.
A Bell & Howell Company
Columbus, Ohio

Standard Book Number 675-09510-7

Library of Congress Catalog Card Number: 69-18904

1 2 3 4 5 6 7 8 9 / 75 74 73 72 71 70 69

Printed in the United States of America

This language scale has been designed for child development specialists, such as psychologists, speech therapists, teachers, and administrators. It can be used with children of all ages who are assumed to be functioning at a preschool or primary language level.

By diagnosing and isolating areas of strengths and deficiencies, this scale will aid in the development and evaluation of language programs.

Irla Lee Zimmerman
Clinical Psychologist

Violette G. Steiner
Child Development Specialist

Roberta L. Evatt
Speech Therapist

Contents

INTRODUCTION

The impetus for this scale came from the authors' observations in Child Development and Cerebral Palsy Preschools. These observations indicated a need for a diagnostic instrument to evaluate developmental progress, maturational lag, strengths and deficiencies in the language skills of young children.

In 1956 Dr. Zimmerman, together with speech therapists and a medical doctor, presented an initial form of a language scale suitable for cerebral palsied infants and children, aged one month to six years. Drawn from the existing developmental literature, this scale attempted a gross differentiation of receptive, expressive, and phonetic skills (D'Asaro, Lehrohoff, Zimmerman, Jones, 1956).

The use of normative development data to produce a language scale has gained increasing acceptance in the last few years. Meacham (1958), soon after the initial report just cited, utilized this approach by drawing from the Vineland (Doll, 1947) and his own experience those items assessing language development. Kinsler in 1966 reported a similar approach, while Doll (1965) used language items in one section of his Preschool Attainment Record, as did Valett (1966) in his Developmental Survey.

None of these authors, however, has separated the auditory and verbal aspects of language skills, nor do they utilize an equal number of items at each age level. The present measure is based upon maturational and developmental aspects of language competence which have been reported by authorities in the fields of normal human development and psycholinguistics.

Unlike other scales which assess language status, this scale uses the natural dichotomy between auditory comprehension and verbal ability as the basis for construction. This allows an assessment of deficiencies which might otherwise be masked or overemphasized by such handicaps as shyness, limited or defective speech, or such pathological problems as asphasia or cerebral palsy. This Preschool Language Scale consists of a series of auditory and verbal language tasks, each

1

of which has been given an age placement on the basis of empirical evidence of the average age of attainment by preschool and early primary children.

All items in this scale have been selected on the psychological premise that a child's auditory comprehension and verbal ability, like all other areas of human ability, develop according to capacity, maturation, and life experiences in a spiraling sequential advancement. The progressive developmental language sequence is important to, must be a part of, and, is indeed, a catalyst for each stage of the child's cognitive, emotional, and psychological development. This appears to be true for the normal child, as well as the cerebral palsied, mentally retarded, deaf, and aphasic child, since each must learn to acquire methods of communicating with others.

It should be stressed here that this scale is not a test, but an evaluation instrument, still in experimental form, to be used to detect language strengths and deficiencies.

GENERAL INSTRUCTIONS

Administration and scoring are two of the most important aspects in the effective use of any evaluative instrument. Carelessness or errors will invalidate the most perceptive interpretation of results. Therefore, it is essential to follow faithfully the specific instructions given in the Manual. Before attempting to administer the Scale, the examiner should become thoroughly familiar with the material described in the Manual, and should practice giving the items.

Testing of young children calls for special skills on the part of the examiner. Easily fatigued and quickly distracted, the preschool child is less motivated than an older child to compete with or surpass others. Testing may need to be temporarily interrupted at evidence of fatigue, negativism or marked inattention. However, the Scale has been composed to elicit maximum performance from the young child; first, by varying the items so that widely differing tasks require only brief responses, and second, by limiting the test to a brief time period (usually well within half an hour) which does not tax the child's attention span.

The most important task of the examiner is to maintain the child's interest and cooperation during the examination. No hard and fast rules can be presented; those who work with young children day by day can usually judge what is likely to elicit the best performance from each child. Good rapport is a prime requisite for a valid test. The child should be given positive reinforcement for his efforts (a smile, a nod, or "very good") whether or not he succeeds. It is important that he have a positive feeling toward the testing situation in order to assure his maximum performance and to preserve a good self-image. While it is important that the child be encouraged to respond, direct help or clues must be avoided. Questions or directions should not be repeated or modified unless so designated in the Manual.

Testing should take place in a comfortable setting, preferably without observers. If the mother's presence is needed to assure cooperation on the part of a younger child, she must be warned to stay in the

background and to say nothing which might suggest an answer to
the child. While this Scale is constructed in English, an interpreter can
be used for children from foreign-language homes, if he is trained not
to change the items by giving some sort of clue, such as frowning,
over-emphasizing key words, looking in the expected direction, or
saying more than the standard instructions.

A number of items occur at more than one age level. Each of these
should be given completely only once. If a child passes an item at one
level, he has automatically passed it at all lower levels. If he fails the
item at a lower level, all subsequent placements of the item are
automatically failed.

Administration

This language evaluation instrument consists of two distinct sections, Auditory Comprehension and Verbal Ability, to be given individually to children assumed to have language skills below seven years.

Each scale is begun by administering the four items at an age level
slightly below the child's estimated ability. If the child misses an item,
the examination has begun at too difficult a level. In such a case, it is
necessary to go back in the scale until the child succeeds in passing
all four items at one age level, which will be the child's basal age.
Testing continues forward from this point. If the child passes any
item at one age level, the following age level must be administered in
full. Each scale is discontinued at the point where the child fails all
items at one age level. Each answer should be recorded in full, allowing further study and evaluation of verbatim responses. This assures
accurate scoring; also, the style of response may prove as meaningful
as the score itself.

Scoring

To score the Preschool Language Scale, the basal age for each
section is entered on the score sheet followed by the number of items
passed at each succeeding level. Those that are between 1 year, 6
months and 5 years are to be multiplied by a credit of 1½ months;
those at 6 and 7 years are multiplied by a credit of 3 months. The
resulting sum is added to the basal age for each section. These age

totals for both the Auditory Comprehension and Verbal Ability Scales represent the equivalent language ages for each.

The Auditory Comprehension age and Verbal Ability age can be compared by converting each to a language quotient. To convert, divide each by the chronological age and multiply by 100 (AQ = ACA ÷ CA × 100; VQ = VAA ÷ CA × 100). An overall language age consists of the average of both Auditory Comprehension and Verbal Ability age (ACA + VAA ÷ 2). This can be converted to a Language Quotient by the same formula: LQ = LA ÷ CA × 100.

MATERIALS

This scale has been carefully devised to eliminate costly and bulky kits. All materials are easily accessible to professional persons working in a school or similar environment.

To administer the Scale, you will need a Preschool Language Scale Booklet for each child to be evaluated, and the following materials:

 1 Preschool Language Scale Manual
 1 Preschool Language Scale Picture Book
12 1" colored blocks (primary colors: red, yellow, green, blue)
 1 Small piece of coarse sandpaper
 1 Set of coins: half-dollar, quarter, dime, nickel, penny
 1 Watch or clock with second hand

AUDITORY COMPREHENSION SCALE

The purpose of the section on Auditory Comprehension is to determine whether the child can receive auditory information, and can indicate this reception by a meaningful, non-verbal response. It provides a measuring instrument to register recognition and comprehension of noun and non-noun words, the stages of concrete and abstract thought, concept acquisition, and the ability to understand grammatical features of the language.

Items have been placed according to a spiraling sequential language progression as indicated by human development specialists such as Gesell, Binet, Terman and Merrill, Piaget, Brown, Van Riper, Templin, Bernstein, and others. In order to succeed, the child must be able to comprehend the task and to respond meaningfully. These receptive skills are a necessary prerequisite in the development of language from auditory perception to vocal production.

This auditory section was carefully designed to preclude the need for any verbalization, thus circumventing such problems as the child who understands, but cannot respond verbally, or who is too shy to do so. A child can understand many words and commands before he can utter them. This fact, at times, confuses those who work with children and who assume such understanding represents equivalent language production. In this scale, a comparison of the performance on the auditory and verbal sections should clarify apparent discrepancies, since a child may have more receptive language ability than can be recognized from his speech, or, on the other hand, may understand far less than children of similar age when his understanding is compared with normative data.

In this scale, vision is used as one of the methods for evaluating language development by requiring the child to identify, manipulate, or conceptualize pictures and objects. Authorities agree that vision is an important component in the development of listening skills and language usage. There is minimal use of motor skills, making the

9

items suitable for administration to the physically handicapped. Auditory Comprehension is a part of all the tasks in this section because listening skills are assessed by items at each developmental stage.

Language development specialists report that this Auditory section provides a valuable instrument for measuring the auditory comprehension level of those children whose speech is impaired or minimal because of pathological or psychological reasons, and may also be of value in assessing a deaf child's ability to read lips. Thus it serves as an excellent instrument for designing language programs or for selecting individual children for speech therapy.

(See the Auditory Comprehension Checklist on page 74.)

AUDITORY COMPREHENSION

1 Year, 6 Months (Four tests, one and one-half months each)

1. RECOGNIZES DOLL PARTS—INDICATES SELF-CONCEPT STRUCTURE (SAME AS 2 YEARS, ITEM NO. 1)

Material: Picture Number 1

Procedure: Say, "Show me the dolly's hair." Repeat for mouth, eyes, feet, nose, ear, hands.

Score: One is passing. The child must definitely point to at least one part on the paper doll as named.

Rationale: Recognition of body parts implies a stage in the development of a child's self-image, which depends on the attention of nurturing adults and on meaningful verbal communication with them.

In order to succeed the child must be able to recognize the auditory word symbol and to respond correctly. For purposes of the Scale, this item is defined as an elementary acquisition stage in the logical sequence of language development, here related to the development of self-image.

Reference: Recognizing body parts was initially used by Binet and Simon (1908) and Terman (1916) at age three. Gesell (1940) located this kind of item at the earlier level starting at 1 year 6 months, as did Cattell (1947).

2. FOLLOWS DIRECTIONS—INDICATES DIFFERENTIATION OF DISTINCTIVES (SAME AS 2 YEARS, ITEM NO. 2)

Material: One block

11

Procedure: The examiner hands the child a block and says, "Put the block on the chair." The block is retrieved, and the child is asked to, "Put the block on the table." The mother or teacher is then warned not to signal in any way, such as by extending her hand, and the child is asked to, "Give the block to mother (teacher)." He is then requested to, "Give the block to me."

Questions may be repeated several times to elicit a response, but at any incorrect response the examiner goes to the next request.

Score: Two is passing. The child must correctly respond to two of the four requests.

Rationale: For a child to carry out simple commands such as these, he must be able to listen attentively, analyze what he has heard, and respond appropriately. Here the child must reveal his comprehension of key words which allow otherwise similar word patterns to represent distinctly differing meanings.

The emphasis at this age is on simple nouns, which are among the first words to be mastered by a child.

Reference: Gesell (1940) used similar instructions with a ball, starting at 1 year, 6 months, and used the item in the Developmental Schedules (1948).

3. Looks Attentively—Indicates FREEDOM FROM DISTRACTABILITY

Material: Picture Number 2

Procedure: Show the picture. Ask the child to look at it and name simple objects, such as the dog, baby, etc. ("Where is the baby?" or "Can you find the baby?")

Score: One is passing. The child must definitely look at and point to at least one picture as named.

Rationale: At this stage the child is mature enough to focus his attention on pictures of familiar objects. The ability to attend and respond to objects, including pictures, is one of the necessary steps in the process of vocabulary building.

At this stage the child is busy understanding and storing auditory verbal symbols. He may or may not have them in his expressive vocabulary. The child no longer uses a book as a manipulative toy, but pauses to look at pictures, an indication that he is beginning to be less susceptible to distraction and can concentrate on more language stimuli.

Reference: Originally utilizing such a situation for "transitional and warming-up purposes," Gesell (1940) found it useful in assessing language. The item was added to the Developmental Schedules (1948).

4. UNDERSTANDS QUESTIONS

Procedure: Say, "Where is mother (teacher, aide)?" "Where is the bathroom?"

Score: One is passing. The child must point or otherwise indicate his knowledge of the question.

Rationale: This item indicates that the child is becoming well-enough acquainted with his environment to make a meaningful (non-verbal) response when questioned. Success indicates the child's developing spatial orientation, as well as his increasing ability to listen and respond to others.

Reference: Gesell (1940, p. 195) summarized the language status of the child at 1 year, 6 months, noting "that he understands and responds to simple directions calling for familiar responses, although reinforcement by gesture is often necessary." Doll (1965) noted that at this age the child uses movement of hands, face, etc., to express understanding.

2 Years (Four tests, one and one-half months each)

1. Recognizes Doll Parts—Indicates SELF-CONCEPT STRUC-
TURE (Same as 1 year, 6 months, item no. 1)

   Material: Picture Number 1

   Procedure: Say, "Show me the dolly's hair." Repeat for mouth, eyes, feet, nose, ear, hands.

   Score: Four is passing. The child must definitely point to at least four parts on the paper doll as named.

   Rationale: Success at this age level indicates a greater awareness of self than was expected at 18 months, and a rapidly increasing vocabulary.

   Reference: Both Binet and Simon (1908), and Terman (1916) had used a three-year placement for such an item. However, in 1937 Terman and Merrill used a recognition of body parts item at this age on both form L and form M, requiring the child to name three parts. In the 1960 revision, Terman and Merrill retained the item, raising the level from three to four, to match the Gesell norms (1940).

2. Follows Directions—Indicates DIFFERENTIATION OF DIS-
TINCTIVES (Same as 1 year, 6 months, item no. 2)

   Material: One block

   Procedure: The examiner hands the child a block and says, "Put the block on the chair." The examiner retrieves the block, and asks the child to "Put the block on the table." The mother or teacher is warned not to signal in any way, such as by extending her hand, and the child is asked to, "Give the block to mother (teacher)." He is then requested to "Give the block to me." The examiner may repeat questions several times to elicit a response, but at any incorrect response, he proceeds to the next request.

   Score: Four is passing.

   Rationale: For the child to carry out these simple commands, he must be able to listen attentively, analyze what he hears, and give an appropriate response. The child must reveal his comprehension of key word distinctions, allowing otherwise similar word patterns to represent different meanings.

At this age a child is able to understand and respond to all four commands, indicating a growing ability to differentiate between nouns.

Reference: Gesell (1940) used similar instructions with a ball and used the item in the Developmental Schedules (1948). Response to commands at this age were also listed by Terman and Merrill (1937).

3. IDENTIFIES PICTURES—INDICATES LABELING RECOGNITION

Material: Picture Number 3

Procedure: Say, "See all these pictures?" "Show me the cup." or "Where is the cup?" or "Put your finger on the cup." Repeat directions for spoon, shoe.

Score: Two is passing. The child must point to two pictures.

Rationale: This item calls for the ability to identify specific pictured objects among a brief array of widely differing objects used daily in a child's life. One of the origins of grammatical structuring is labeling recognition ability.

Reference: The response to pictures has been prominent in testing for years. Gesell (1940) noted that children could point to five or more pictures from a ten-picture assortment at this age. Haeussermann (1958) presented simple pictures of objects common in children's environments. Doll (1965) noted ability to *discriminate* or *identify* at this age. Terman and Merrill (1937) required children to point to parts of a doll and to point to minature objects as named; both items are retained in the 1960 version.

4. DISCRIMINATES PICTURES—INDICATES DIFFERENTIAL CLASSIFICATION

Material: Pictures Number 4 and 5

Procedure: Say, "Where is the dog?" or "Which one is the dog?" or "Point to the dog." Repeat for wagon.

Score: Two is passing. The child must point correctly to both.

Rationale: Ability to discriminate between two similar objects is a necessary step in vocabulary acquisition. At this age, a child's auditory vocabulary should allow him to recognize the object or animal called for, and to distinguish each one from members of the same class.

Reference: Taylor (1965) noted the selective scanning of pictures at age two; Terman and Merrill (1937, 1960) limited this to finding parts of the body. Doll (1965) reported that children at two years of age "discriminate" and make simple judgments in differentiation.

2 Years, 6 Months (Four tests, one and one-half months each)

1. UNDERSTANDS THE CONCEPT OF THE NUMBER "ONE"—INDICATES QUANTITATIVE COMPREHENSION

Material: Twelve blocks

Procedure: Say, "Give me just one."

Score: One is passing. The child must hand one block to the examiner. If this is followed by one or more, the item is failed.

Rationale: A correct response to this item presupposes that the child grasps the essential meaning of the verbal symbol "one" and has the ability to apply this concept to a new set of objects. This association will be critical in the development of mathematical comprehension and logical reasoning.

Reference: Gesell (1940) reported that children have mastered the concept of "one" at this age level, and Cattell (1947) added this concept to her items at age two.

2. COMPARES SIZE (I)—INDICATES SIZE CONSERVATION

Material: Picture Number 6

Procedure: Say, "Show me the tiny, little spoon."

Score: One is passing. The child must point to the smaller spoon on the first trial.

Rationale: The ability to differentiate size indicates an advancing language comprehension and understanding of verbal adjectives. At this age level, similar objects can be distinguished from each other on the basis of one pertinent characteristic—in this case, size. This item also has application to the development of numerical skills.

Reference: The ability of children at this age to discriminate size in extreme cases was noted by Gesell (1948). Haeussermann (1958) presented similar material at age two and one-half years.

3. UNDERSTANDS USE (I)—INDICATES ENVIRONMENTAL OBJECT
   EXPERIENCE (SAME AS 3 YEARS, ITEM NO. 3)

Material: Picture Number 7

Procedure: Say, "Show me what. . . ." or
              "Which is the one that. . . . .?"

          a. "we use to comb our hair"
          b. "we use to drink our milk"
          c. "goes on our feet"
          d. "we ride on"
          e. "we use to iron clothes"
          f. "we can cut with"
          g. "we use to sweep the floor"

Score: Two is passing. The child must point to the designated
              picture. Naming without correctly pointing receives no
              credit.

Rationale: At this age level, a child is able to identify pictures of
              familiar objects when they are described in terms of
              their use.
                  Success at this level indicates an advancing language
              comprehension, beyond the previous stage of identifying
              pictured objects only by name. The understanding that
              function as well as label describes an object is a begin-
              ning stage in the concept of relationships among specific
              features of his physical environment. An important factor
              in the development of language lies in the construction
              of relationships beyond simple identification.

Reference: Gesell (1940) found children able to give the use for at
              least one of the objects he asked them to name (key),
              and placed this sort of item on the Developmental
              Schedules (1948). Terman and Merrill (1937, 1960) used
              the miniature objects and the present form; the child was
              required to point to the object which matched the use
              named. Haeussermann (1958) found children able to
              distinguish pictures when their use was named, and
              Taylor (1958) placed this skill at the same age.

4. FOLLOWS SIMPLE COMMANDS—INDICATES OPERATIONAL COR-
   RESPONDENCE

Material: Twelve blocks, box

Procedure: Say,

   a. "Make a tower like this." (Build a four-block tower.) "Good!"
   b. "Now let's make a train!" (Line up four blocks in a row, adding one on top of the first, and push the blocks, saying, "Choo-choo-choo!") "You do it." "Good!"
   c. "Now put the blocks in the box."

Score: Two is passing. The child must stack four or more blocks to make a tower, put three or more blocks in a line and push them, and/or put more than half the blocks into the box. (He may need encouragement).

Rationale: By the time the child reaches this stage of language development, he has had various kinds and degrees of auditory and verbal experiences with his environment. He has discovered many of the regularities of the language, and uses this skill to understand and respond to requests of adults. Through completion of this task, the child demonstrates his visual-motor coordination, his comprehension of the task, and a memory span sufficient to hold one familiar direction long enough to imitate another's actions. This ability to imitate is one of the early developmental stages of cognitive learning, and a stepping-stone toward the development of operational correspondence.

Reference: Terman and Merrill (1937) had a series of similar commands at this age level. Cattell (1947) used these commands individually at approximately this age level.

3 Years (Four tests, one and one-half months each)

1. RECOGNIZES ACTION—INDICATES ACTIVITY SENTENCING DIS-
CRIMINATION

Material: Picture Number 8

Procedure: Say, "Where are the children washing?"
              "Where are the children playing?"

Score: Two is passing. The child must differentiate between two
              kinds of action.

Rationale: This item calls for comprehension of a more advanced
              type of sentence structure. The distinguishing character-
              istic of the questions involves discrimination between
              single words in the sentences and visual discrimination
              of pictures.
                  This item is particularly valuable in evaluating lan-
              guage of deprived children. Some research (Dunn, 1959)
              has suggested that this verb form is difficult for them to
              master.

Reference: Gesell (1940) required that children name action in
              pictures; in the Developmental Schedules (1948) the
              same item was used. Haeussermann (1958) required
              children to distinguish portrayed action at this age level,
              and this is the form used here.

2. DISTINGUISHES PREPOSITIONS—INDICATES PREPOSITIONAL DIS-
TINCTIVES (SAME AS 4 YEARS, ITEM NO. 2)

Material: One block

Procedure: Say, "Put this block. . . ."
              "Can you put the block. . . . .?"
              a. "on the chair"
              b. "under the chair"
              c. "in front of the chair"
              d. "beside the chair"
              e. "in back of the chair"

Score: Two is passing. The child must correctly follow two
              commands.

Rationale: Children at this age should have mastered two of these simple prepositions. Such mastery is necessary if the child is to understand and to use the language. The only differentiation between the sentences included in this item are the prepositions, their appearance signaling a sharp change of meaning. These prepositions are a form of what Piaget (1963) calls *distinctives*, and, as research indicates, the last parts of speech to be included in a child's language comprehension. These abstract grammatical distinctives now have stability and the child is able to adapt the verbal symbols to various situations. The child can now use this framework to separate, distinguish, and adapt the verbal symbols to various situations.

Reference: Gesell (1940, 1948) found children had mastered two of these simple prepositions.

3. UNDERSTANDS USE (I)—INDICATES ENVIRONMENTAL OBJECT EXPERIENCE (SAME AS 2 YEARS, 6 MONTHS, ITEM NO. 3)

Material: Picture Number 7

Procedure: Say, "Show me what. . ." or "Which is the one that. . .?"
   a. "we use to comb our hair"
   b. "we use to drink our milk"
   c. "goes on our foot"
   d. "we ride on"
   e. "we use to iron our clothes"
   f. "we can cut with"
   g. "we use to sweep the floor"

Score: Four is passing. The child must point to the designated picture. Naming without correct pointing receives a minus score.

Rationale: At this age level, a child is able to identify a greater number of pictures of familiar objects than at the earlier testing level, when the objects are described in terms of their use.
   The child is increasing his store of information, his ability to classify both noun and non-noun words, and also his capability for learning specific communicative operations.

Reference: This format is similar to that used by Terman and
                 Merrill (1937), where five out of six objects must be cor-
                 rectly identified.

4. DISTINGUISHES PARTS—INDICATES DIFFERENTIAL PART-WHOLE
   CLASSIFICATION

Material: Picture Number 9

Procedure: Say, "Where are the wheels of the car?"
                 "Where is the tail of the horse?"

Score: Two is passing. The child must differentiate between
                 pictures and point to the correct area of each picture.

Rationale: To succeed on this item, the child must first be able to
                 discriminate between general categories and then be-
                 tween two members of the same class. Then he can
                 identify the specific part called for. Such attention to
                 differential detail is a stage in the development of ability
                 to classify.

Reference: This item is based on the work of Taylor (1959), who
                 noted ability to distinguish pertinent parts of pictures at
                 this age. Gesell (1940) mentioned ability to analyze
                 pictures, based on the 1916 Binet item (Terman, 1916).

3 Years, 6 Months (Four tests, one and one-half months each)

1. RECOGNIZES TIME—INDICATES TEMPORAL ORDERING

Material: Picture Number 11

Procedure: Say, "Which one tells you it is nighttime?"

Score: One is passing. The child must point to the correct picture on the first trial.

Rationale: This is a beginning step in the child's ability to understand the sequential passage of time. He now understands major concepts of time, such as day and night, on the basis of the different activities which are appropriate to each.

Reference: This item is based on Haeussermann (1958) who noted ability to differentiate between pictured time periods.

2. COMPARES SIZE (II)—INDICATES SIZE CONSERVATION

Material: Picture Number 12

Procedure: Say, "Show me the long one." or "Put your finger on the long line."

Present the picture three times, alternating the relative position of the lines. If one of the first three trials is failed, continue with three additional trials.

Score: Three correct responses out of three trials or five out of six trials is a passing score.

Rationale: Success here indicates that the child understands the distinction between minor size differences. Terman and Merrill (1937, p. 203) noted that an item such as this "probably gauges language comprehension rather than actual discrimination of length."

Because of the child's increasing awareness of minute differences, this item also has application to the development of numerical skills.

Reference: This form of the item was in the first Binet (Binet and Simon, 1908). Terman and Merrill (1937, 1960) used sticks instead of lines, and noted that children are able to distinguish between these relatively small differences at this age level. Gesell (1940), on the other hand, noted this at age four.

3. MATCHES SETS—INDICATES OPERATIONAL CORRESPONDENCE

Material: Twelve blocks

Procedure: Take one block, place it on a piece of paper, and say, "Look what I have put here." "You take one and put it there." After the child has complied, replace both blocks.

            Take four blocks, place them about an inch apart, and say, "Now look what I have on my paper." "You take that many too." Do the same with two blocks, saying, "Now like this." Repeat with three blocks, saying, "Now this many."

Score: Three is passing. Child must match the exact number of blocks for three of the four responses.

Rationale: For a child to understand the concept of quantity, he needs to see a group as a measurable whole made up of separate related items. This concept develops as the child learns to match groups of objects, one-to-one. The development of the ability to match the visual image in operational correspondence is one of the early prerequisites for competence in learning to read.

            This task proves to be a good measure of a child's attention span and his freedom from distraction. It also calls for comprehension of verbal directions and visual acuity.

Reference: Terman and Merrill (1937) listed a similar item, while Gesell's Developmental Schedules (1948) noted that a child can imitate a structure of blocks presented by the examiner.

4. GROUPS OBJECTS—INDICATES CLASSIFICATION INTEGRATION

Material: Picture Number 13

Procedure: Say, "Show me. . . ." or
                   "See if you can find all. . . . ."
           a. "the animals"
           b. "the things we eat"
           c. "the toys"

    Score: Two is passing. The child must point to three or more pictures in a group.

   Rationale: This task involves the ability to select and assign objects to a class without distraction from the overall goal. This item indicates a child's comprehension of class, ability to categorize, and language comprehension, as well as his ability to sustain attention.

   Reference: Taylor (1958) noted that children could succeed in selecting objects by groups.

4 Years (Four tests, one and one-half months each)

1. RECOGNIZES COLORS—INDICATES COLOR RECOGNITION (SAME
   AS 4 YEARS, 6 MONTHS, ITEM NO. 1)

   Material: Four colored blocks

   Procedure: Say, "Show me . . ." or "Point to. . . . ."
           a. "the RED block"
           b. "the BLUE block"
           c. "the YELLOW block"
           d. "the GREEN block"

   Score: One is passing.

   Rationale: Knowledge of colors indicates the child's increasing ability to classify and organize elements of his environment.
   Early mastery of concepts such as color is one of the
   bases upon which a child develops his ability to perform
   categorical grouping.

   Reference: Doll (1965) mentioned that selecting or identifying
   colors comes earlier than the ability to name them.
   Gesell (1940) noted that at four years of age children
   can readily name one color, while only 41% can name
   two. Hence, the requirement for recognition alone is
   placed at four years.

2. DISTINGUISHES PREPOSITIONS—INDICATES PREPOSITIONAL DIS-
   TINCTIVES (SAME AS 3 YEARS, ITEM NO. 2)

   Material: One block

   Procedure: Say, "Put this block. . . ." or
           "Can you put the block. . . . ?"
           a. "on the chair"
           b. "under the chair"
           c. "in front of the chair"
           d. "beside the chair"
           e. "in back of the chair"

   Score: Four is passing. The child must correctly follow four
   commands.

Rationale: At this stage the child must have the linguistic competence to understand and respond to more prepositional distinctives than was expected at three years. Such competence is necessary if the child is to understand the detailed workings of language. He has, by now, expanded his framework for separating, distinguishing, and adapting verbal symbols.

Reference: By age four, Gesell (1940) found the child to know a number of prepositions.

3. Differentiates Texture—Indicates TACTILE COMPREHENSION

Material: Sandpaper and paper with smooth surface

Procedure: Say, "See this? Feel this. Feel the paper. Which is smoother? Which is rougher?"

Score: Two is passing. The child must answer both correctly at the first trial.

Rationale: The child who is successful on this item has further gained a sense of regularity and stability in the world around him. He is capable of making sensory discrimination, has learned to grasp relationships, to classify, and to understand the tactile, abstract concept of "smoother." This continuing use of all his senses as a means of learning about his environment allows the child to conceptualize, through recognition of similarity between verbal symbols, understanding of their meanings, and comprehending and/or communicating with others.

Reference: Haeussermann (1958) noted tactile sensitivity at this age, and Doll (1965) reported that children were able to understand gross comparisons requiring the sense of touch.

4. Understands Use (II)—Indicates CONCEPT ACQUISITION (Same as 4 years, 6 months, item no. 4)

Material: Picture Number 14

Procedure: Say, "Show me which one . . . Find the one that. . . . ."
    a. "swims in the water"
    b. "tells time"

      c. "we write with"
      d. "we read"
      e. "we eat at"
      f. "we put two pieces of wood together with"
      g. "we cut with"

Score: Five is passing.

Rationale: This item calls for fairly wide knowledge of concepts outside a child's immediate environment. As such, it gives a measure of the verbal contact the child has had with adults, and suggests the degree of curiosity and successful communication experiences with pictures and words.

References: Terman and Merrill (1937, 1960) place a similar item at four years; Gesell (1940) mentioned such an item with only two successes.

4 Years, 6 Months (Four tests, one and one-half months each)

1. RECOGNIZES COLORS—INDICATES COLOR RECOGNITION (SAME AS 4 YEARS, ITEM NO. 1)

Material: Four colored blocks

Procedure: Say, "Show me. . . ." or "Point to. . . . ."
        a. "the RED block"
        b. "the BLUE block"
        c. "the YELLOW block"
        d. "the GREEN block"

Score: Four is passing.

Rationale: At this age, a child should be able to recognize all the primary colors. (See Rationale, 4 years, item no. 1, p. 26)

Reference: Gesell (1940) noted that by four years 41% of his sample could name two, but by this age children can recognize most primary colors as named for them.

2. TOUCHES THUMBS—INDICATES DIFFERENTIATION OF SELF

Procedure: Say, "Place your left thumb against your right thumb."

Score: One is passing. The child must touch thumbs at the first trial.

Rationale: The ability to differentiate and respond to directions with both sides of the body suggests that the child is developing an understanding and mastery of himself. The ability to perform a double command is a task requiring attention to verbal language, a degree of motor coordination, and willingness to respond actively to adult commands.

Reference: Ilg and Ames (1964) noted almost complete success at five and one-half (95%), so the median age for success is at this earlier level.

3. UNDERSTANDS THE CONCEPT OF THE NUMBER "THREE"—INDICATES QUANTITATIVE COMPREHENSION

Material: Twelve blocks

Procedure: Say, "Give me just three." or "Can you give me just three?"

Score: One is passing. The child must hand three blocks to the examiner. If one or more follows, the item is failed.

Rationale: At this age, the child should have had sufficient experience with multiple objects and the concept of quantity to understand numbers. The child has not merely added the word "three" to his vocabulary, but now grasps the essential relationship between the verbal symbol and the constant quantity of "three" (three of anything).

   This development of conservation of quantity is the necessary condition for the growth of language, logical reasoning, and abstract thinking.

Reference: Gesell (1940) noted children could adaptively place or give three blocks at this age.

4. UNDERSTANDS USE (II)—INDICATES CONCEPT ACQUISITION (SAME AS 4 YEARS, ITEM NO. 4)

Material: Picture Number 14

Procedure: Say, "Show me which one. . . ." or
                  "Find the one that. . . ."
               a. "swims in the water"
               b. "tells time"
               c. "we write with"
               d. "we read"
               e. "we eat at"
               f. "we put two pieces of wood together with"
               g. "we cut with"

Score: Seven is passing.

Rationale: At this level, a child can comprehend and thus correctly respond to more questions than at four years of age, revealing a growing breadth of vocabulary and skill in classification.

Reference: A similar item appears at this age level both in Terman and Merrill (1937, 1960) and Gesell (1940).

5 Years (Four tests, one and one-half months each)

1. COMPREHENDS RIGHT—INDICATES DIFFERENTIATION OF SELF

Procedure: Say, "Show me your right hand." (Ask a second time after an intervening item.)

Score: Two is passing. The child must correctly identify his right hand.

Rationale: This item requires the child to differentiate between the left and right sides of his body. It is one of the first stages in the growth of directional orientation and indicates a continuing development in the child's differentiation of self.

One of the important implications here is the meaning of direction and the child's underlying intellectual orientation with his environment.

Reference: Ilg and Ames (1964) found such a task mastered between five and five and one-half years of age.

2. TAPS RHYTHM—INDICATES ATTENTIVE AUDITORY IMITATION

Procedure: Say, "Tap the table just like I do. Listen carefully and wait until I finish tapping before you start."
   a. Tap twice.
   b. Tap four times.
   c. Tap three times.
   Tap evenly the number of times indicated, with intervals of approximately one second between taps

Score: Two is passing.

Rationale: This item is a measure of simple auditory discrimination, but, unlike digit span, there is no need for a verbal response. Success involves temporal and auditory perceptual organization and has been considered a factor in predicting school achievement. Difficulty here may be a clue to auditory disorders.

Reference: Arthur (1947) noted the ability to repeat patterns on the Knox Cubes at this age level. Doll (1965) placed beating rhythm at six years. De Hirsch (1966) mentioned tapping success at this age.

3. DISTINGUISHES WEIGHT DIFFERENCES—INDICATES CONSERVATION OF SIZE

Material: Picture Number 15

Procedure: Say, "Show me the one which is heavier. . ." or
"Point to the one which is heavier. . ."
  a. "a bird or a cow"
  b. "a bed or a chair"
  c. "a boot or a shoe"
  d. "a car or a dump truck"
  e. "a lock or a leaf"

Score: Four is passing. The child must discriminate correctly between four pairs.

Rationale: A child's formation of concepts follows a developmental pattern closely related to his auditory, verbal, visual, and life experiences. To succeed in this task, the child must have acquired the concept of the abstract word *heavier* and apply it in a meaningful and useful way. The item indicates whether or not the child is capable of retaining and applying information gained in other situations to solve problems. A child must develop a measure of inner (schematic) safeguards against perceptual illusion in order to acquire a relevant vocabulary and to achieve stable and consistent usage of that vocabulary.

Reference: Doll (1965) noted that children can differentiate relative differences in weight, as between light and heavy (at least at gross levels), at the age of five. Gesell (1940, 1948) noted success in differentiating weights using the two-block test, with one block weighing three grams and the other weighing fifteen grams.

4. KNOWS BODY PARTS—INDICATES SELF CONCEPT

Procedure: Say, "Show me your head." Repeat for arm, hand, knee, heel, eyebrow, little finger, elbow, palm, chin.

Score: Eight is passing. The child must point correctly to eight of the ten body parts named.

Rationale: Since self-concept is difficult to measure, an assumption is made that a child's interest in and knowledge of the vocabulary which identifies his body parts is indicative of good self-image. This item measures subtly the degree of interest a child has experienced with a concerned and stimulating adult. The better his sense of self, the more able he is to observe and be aware of the world around him. Thus, his self-knowledge allows him freedom to use himself as a tool in assessing his environment.

Reference: Ilg and Ames (1964) used the knowledge of body parts, noting that by age five, over 50% could name the parts; hence, a greater percentage could recognize parts such as these.

6 Years (Four tests, three months each)

1. COMPREHENDS DIRECTIONAL COMMANDS (I)—INDICATES DIFFER-
ENTIATION OF SELF

Procedure: Say, "Put your left hand on your left knee."

Score: One is passing. The child must respond correctly on the
first trial.

Rationale: Ability to manipulate both sides of the body in following
directions suggests that the child has developed real
understanding of his body. This is a more advanced concept of differentiation of self. To succeed in the task, the
child must differentiate both sides of his body, and can
use this skill in spatial orientation.

Reference: Ilg and Ames (1964) found that by age six, children
could succeed on double commands such as this. Gesell
(1948) mentioned knowledge of right and left at six
years.

2. COUNTS BLOCKS—INDICATES CONCEPT OF QUANTITY

Material: Twelve blocks

Procedure: Place blocks in a pile near the child and say, "Can you
put three blocks here?" Repeat for nine blocks; five
blocks; seven blocks.

Score: Three is passing.

Rationale: This item requires a knowledge of the seriation of numbers. However, the most important factor is that the
child has a concept of stability of quantity and its relationship to seriation. This concept is a necessary condition for the advancement of mathematical understanding
and a prerequisite for the development of logical reasoning.

Reference: Terman and Merrill (1937, 1960) listed block counting
at this age. Gesell (1940) quoted the earlier Binet
(1916), and mentioned several forms of counting.

3. Distinguishes Animal Parts—Indicates CLASSIFICATION CONCEPT

Material: Picture Number 16

Procedure: Say, "Which one has. . . ?"
   a. "the longest nose"
   b. "a bushy tail"
   c. "pointed ears"
   d. "a long, thin tail"

Score: Four is passing. The child must name all four correctly.

Rationale: This item indicates that the child has added descriptive adjectives to his auditory vocabulary and is able to use them as a classification tool. This vocabulary change indicates the child's advancing cognitive development and his understanding of the essential concept of each distinctive word. In this case, adjectives are the distinctive words.

Reference: Taylor (1959) noted that children of six were able to identify animals by differential questions.

4. Adds Numbers up to Five—Indicates ABSTRACT COMPUTATION

Procedure: Say, "If you have one penny and I give you one more penny, how many will you have?"
   "If you have two pennies and I give you two more pennies, how many will you have?"
   "If you have three pennies and I give you two more pennies, how many will you have?"

Score: Two is passing. The child must respond to two of the three questions. Gestures, such as holding up fingers, are acceptable.

Rationale: This item indicates a child's understanding of simple mathematical concepts. Ability to complete the task without seeing or handling the actual objects requires abstract thought.

Reference: Gesell (1940, 1948) noted that children can add and subtract within the first five numbers at this age.

7 Years (Four tests, three months each)

1. COMPREHENDS DIRECTIONAL COMMANDS (II)—INDICATES DIFFER-
ENTIATION OF SELF

Procedure: Say, "Touch your right thumb with your right little
finger."

Score: One is passing. The child must respond correctly at the
first trial.

Rationale: This item requires the ability to differentiate between the
right and left sides of the body and to follow a double
command. This task is more difficult than the item
requiring a gross identification of right and left, since it
requires also a certain amount of manual dexterity to
achieve success. The child must also recognize the verbal
symbols which indicate specific parts of his body, namely
his hands, thus indicating further growth in the concept
of self-differentiation.

This item provides a clue to the child's maturational
level of eye-hand-motor coordination, which is one of the
salient symptomatic features of writing skill, and shows
the child's feeling of security in self-motor control. This
control and differentiation of self is one of the variety
of abilities involved in continuing development of language skills.

Reference: Ilg and Ames (1964) found children at age seven could
succeed at double commands such as this one.

2. COUNTING TAPS—INDICATES AUDITORY ACUITY

Procedure: Say, "Listen!" Tap twice on the table with a pencil.
"How many times did I tap?" Repeat as necessary, until
the child responds correctly. "How many this time?"
   a. Tap seven times.
   b. Tap five times.
   c. Tap eight times.

Score: Three is passing. The child must correctly respond to all
three, but need not verbalize the response if he is shy or

non-verbal. Tapping, holding up fingers, or pointing, are acceptable responses.

Rationale: An important factor here is the child's ability to store in his memory an auditory pattern of this length. When the child makes the correct number of taps, he links this auditory memory with the necessary pattern of activity. Thus he arrives at a satisfactory response through his auditory acuity.

Reference: Kuhlman (1922) and Terman and Merrill (1937) are among the examiners who have utilized this kind of item.

3. COIN VALUES—INDICATES CONCEPT OF QUANTITY

Material: Picture Number 17 and coins (dime, nickel, quarter, half dollar)

Procedure: Say, "Look at this money. Can you tell me how many pennies are in a . . . ?"
  a. "dime"
  b. "nickel"
  c. "quarter"
  d. "half dollar"
The child may point to a written representation of the correct number.

Score: Three is passing. The child can spontaneously point to the correct value, or name the number of pennies.

Rationale: Success here calls for knowledge and social experience with important objects in his environment. This data is an indication of the child's underlying orientation with his environment and some of its functional aspects. It shows that his communicative experiences have provided some specific concrete mathematical understanding. His concept of the interrelationship between coins and their numerical value is now stable in his thoughts. This is one of the aspects necessary for gaining knowledge of sets, and for logical thinking. He can also communicate his concept of specific quantity to adults.

Reference: Gesell (1940) mentioned children's knowledge of this information by age seven.

4. Adds and Subtracts numbers up to Ten—Indicates OPERATIONAL CORRESPONDENCE

Material: Picture Number 17

Procedure: Say, "If you had ten pennies and gave away four, how many would you have?"

"If you had five pennies and I gave you five more, how many would you have?"

"If you had five pennies and lost one, how many would you have?"

Score: Two is passing. The child must respond to two of the three questions. Gestures, such as holding up fingers, are acceptable responses.

Rationale: Success with this item indicates that the child has a knowledge of the definitions of terms, has a memory span sufficient to maintain the verbal task long enough to examine the problem, and has reached the stage where he comprehends the correspondence between object sets and the numbers used to count them. Numbers, for him, have a continuous quantity which can be used in reasoning. The necessary operations are logically established, and he has enough available language to enable him to return an accurate verbal response.

Reference: Gesell (1940) report ability to add and subtract primary numbers by this age.

Verbal Ability Scale

The Verbal Ability section of this scale will help determine whether a child can verbalize adequately, as measured by his responses to a series of graded tasks. It provides an instrument for measuring such aspects as vocabulary (word availability), verbalized memory span, stages of concrete and abstract thought, concept acquisition, articulation, and ability to use grammatical features of the language.

Items have been arranged according to the same spiraling sequential language progression as are the tasks of the Auditory Comprehension Scale. In order to succeed, the child must be able both to comprehend the task and to respond verbally. These verbal skills are the natural outcome in the development of language from auditory perception to vocal production.

This verbal section will elicit a variety of oral responses. This approach allows the diagnosis of such problems as the child who is verbally fluent without real understanding. Some children may show considerable verbal fluency or specific skill in articulation without corresponding comprehension. Others are so limited by articulation or linguistic deficits that they are unable to communicate adequately, and their basic language comprehension is overlooked. In this scale, general language skills can be compared in terms of non-verbal and verbal production.

Language development specialists report that, since this verbal scale allows an assessment of the various skills involved in language fluency and use, it is of great value for determining the content of language programs and selecting children for individual speech therapy.

(See the Verbal Ability Checklist on page 76.)

Verbal Ability

1 Year, 6 Months (Four tests, one and one-half months each)

1. Uses Ten Words—Indicates VERBAL FLUENCY

Procedure: Observation or report. If an extensive list of words is not reported by the mother or another individual who knows the child, ask specifically for "no," "yes," "hello," "bye-bye," "car," "go," and other common early words. Ask whether the child has names for persons, toys, animals, food, and so forth.

Score: Ten is passing. The child is observed or reported to use ten or more words, including names. Disregard faulty pronunciation.

Rationale: This item is one measure of progression from the babbling stage to the use of verbal symbols, and indicates how rapidly a child is replacing jargon with spoken words. During this stage, the child must acquire the concept that a particular verbal symbol represents a specific object. These words must be used consistently and appropriately for the same objects and persons.

    Without these initially attained words, there is no basis for the rapidly expanding, meaningful vocabulary and linguistic competence that must be developed in the preschool period. Recent studies in psycholinguistics generally agree that grammatical structure begins at about 1 year, 6 months, and that the foundation for competence in adult grammar has normally been completed at about 3 years, 6 months.

41

Reference: At 1 year, 6 months, the average child reveals a rapidly
                 expanding vocabulary. Smith (1926) had reported this
                 degree of language development from mothers' diaries.
                 Gesell (1940) listed ten words at this age and added this
                 item to the Developmental Schedules (1948).

2. NAMES ONE PICTURE—INDICATES AVAILABLE VOCABULARY FOR LABELING

Material: Picture Book

Procedure: Present simple pictures, such as dog, shoe, etc. Say,
                 "What is this?" or "What do you call this?"

Score: One is passing. The child must name one or more objects
                 familiar to him. Disregard faulty pronunciation.

Rationale: Since the child has the ability to recognize many objects
                 long before he can name them, this item reveals the
                 beginning availability of words. This availability is
                 directly related to the initial labeling activities which are
                 a necessary part of *vocal encoding*. In order for a child
                 to learn to label objects, Kirk (1940) pointed out that he
                 must be able to identify their salient features. Hence,
                 this item also measures his ability to attend to objects,
                 such as pictures, long enough to recognize their familiar
                 elements.
                     Gesell (1948) noted that a child at 1 year, 6 months
                 shows an active interest in books, looks at pictures selec-
                 tively, and no longer uses books as a manipulative toy.

Reference: Gesell (1948) found that children could identify two or
                 more pictures by naming or pointing.

3. ASKS FOR SIMPLE NEED—INDICATES VERBAL NEED COMMUNICATION

Procedure: Observation or report. Can ask for "water," "milk,"
                 "more," or the like.

Score: One is passing. The child is observed or reported to use
                 regularly at least one word to express a need. Disregard
                 faulty pronunciation.

Rationale: This item calls for more than random speech, and in-
                 volves the use of simple words for direct communication.

The most important factor here is that these single words form a base language structure. They form a sentence to the child, even though each word is subject to different interpretations. For example, when a child says, "milk," the interpretation may be, "Please give me some milk." Thus, this item has been used to indicate the beginning of grammatical speech.

The manipulation of language to meet personal needs means that language usage will be increasingly rewarded and reinforced. The child is now able to understand and express internal needs so that, to some extent, he can control and manipulate his environment. The child's sense of self and his significance to others in his world is thus enhanced.

Reference: Cattell (1947) noted the ability of children to ask for "more" at this age level, while Gesell (1940) mentioned the beginning communication that this item implies.

4. ECHOES OR IMITATES—INDICATES VERBAL IMITATION

Procedure: Observation. Imitates or echoes sounds or words, such as "kitty," "dinner," with repetitive or playful urging.

Score: Two is passing. The child must imitate at least two different words or sounds.

Rationale: This item involves attention to and interest in imitative verbal symbolization. In the child's attempt to learn new words, he is able to identify himself with others. The ability to imitate is an important activity in the development of speech. Only through discrimination of sounds does a child begin to master verbal language. Its absence may be an indication of a hearing loss, lack of stimulation, or lack of opportunity for practice.

In addition to this labeling facility and visual imagery, this item requires both attention and memory, in that the child must retain an auditory impression long enough to reproduce it.

Reference: Stutsman (1931) listed specific words which her sample of children could repeat at 1 year, 6 months, while Doll (1965) broadened the item to include other forms of imitation.

2 Years (Four tests, one and one-half months each)

1. COMBINES WORDS—INDICATES EARLY GRAMMATICAL SEN-
   TENCING

Procedure: Observation. The child's vocabulary is extended by
                simple phrases and noun-verb combinations used spon-
                taneously at any time during the interview.

Score: Two is passing. The child must combine two or more
            words appropriately, using two different word combina-
            tions. ("Where mama?" "See car.") Mere echoing is not
            acceptable.

Rationale: This is a step in the development of organized language
                patterns and is an advance over word combinations such
                as "allgone," which is essentially a one-word usage.

                At two years of age, the child has acquired verbal
                symbols which differentiate certain aspects of his en-
                vironment. He now begins to combine words in order to
                acquire information and to further understand and con-
                trol his world. It also indicates an increased memory span
                and elementary (primitive) grammatical sentence struc-
                turing, since words chosen are from two grammatical
                classes and are not random responses.

Reference: McCarthy (1930) reported the mean number of words
                per response at this age as 1.8, while both Terman and
                Merrill (1937, 1960) and Gesell (1940, 1948) noted two
                or more word sentences.

2. NAMES OBJECTS IN ENVIRONMENT—INDICATES CONCRETE OB-
   JECT LABELING (SAME AS 2 YEARS, 6 MONTHS, ITEM NO. 2)

Procedure: Ask "What is that?" pointing in turn to nearby objects:
                shoe, watch, table, ball, chair, block, pencil, floor

Score: Three is passing.

Rationale: Success at this point indicates that the child shows ex-
                perience with and interest in his environment and can
                identify and label most of its simple concrete elements.
                Many of his verbal symbols now have consistent meaning

for both speaker and listener. Success at the task also suggests that he is actively orienting himself to his listener and to his environment, and gives further evidence that the child is continuing to add words to his vocabulary.

Reference: Gesell (1940) noted children at age two could name two objects; on the Developmental Schedules (1948) he used ability to name pictures. Terman and Merrill (1937, 1960) listed both pictures and objects named at this age.

3. Uses Pronouns—Indicates DIFFERENTIATION OF SELF

Procedure: Observation or report. Note whether *I, me, you* are differentiated (although *I* and *me* are often confused).

Score: One is passing. The child must be observed or reported to use one or more pronouns correctly. Acceptable: colloquialisms such as "I's is," "Us's is."

Rationale: Success here indicates that the child is mastering the *reciprocal relationship* existing among the pronouns *I, me,* and *you.* Although these pronouns have been within the child's auditory and verbal range of ability for some time, he is now learning their relationship to himself and other people. The most important factor is the child's use of first person pronouns in place of his own name. To understand that *I* can be *you* as well, means that the child can see himself from another's viewpoint and, hence, has a heightened sense of self-differentiation. This linguistic skill gives the child another means of differentiating himself from others.

Reference: Gesell (1940, p. 198) noted that the use of pronouns at age two was "the most conspicuous development in the matter of parts of speech."

4. Refers to Self by Name—Indicates SELF CONCEPT

Procedure: Observation or report. Note whether the child tells of his activities calling himself by name. ("Jimmy do it." "Sally go home!")

Score: One is passing. The child must be observed or reported to use his own first name at least once. Ignore faulty pronunciation.

Rationale: A child's ability and interest in verbalizing his activities
and his pride in discussing his accomplishments is ac-
companied by use of his own name. It also indicates that
he is incorporating his own linguistic skill to help identify
his role and the concept of himself as an individual.

This stage is congruent with the initial use of pronouns.
Within six months the average child advances to consistent use of a pronoun instead of his own name, another
step in the stage of self-understanding.

Reference: The tendency of children at this age to refer to them-
selves by name in their conversations was noted by Gesell
(1940, 1948).

2 Years, 6 Months (Four tests, one and one-half months each)

1. REPEATS TWO DIGITS—INDICATES ATTENTIVE VERBAL IMITA-TION

Procedure: Say, "Listen: say 2. Now say: 4–7; 5–8; 3–9." The numbers must be pronounced uniformly and distinctly at the rate of one per second.

Score: One is passing. The child must repeat one of the series in correct order. Ignore faulty pronunciation.

Rationale: The ability to listen actively is an important facet of communication. Attention is essential to learning; it contributes to the child's stock of ideas. To gain competence in listening skills and ability in reproducing verbal symbols, the child must be able to attend actively to auditory stimuli and to remember those stimuli long enough to imitate them.

Anderson (1953) noted that when memory span is delayed in maturing, speech development is also likely to be retarded.

Reference: Digit span memory for digits was drawn from the 1916 Binet (Terman, 1916) by Gesell (1940, 1948) and was used again in all subsequent forms of the Binet (1937, 1960).

2. NAMES OBJECTS IN ENVIRONMENT—INDICATES CONCRETE OB-JECT LABELING (SAME AS 2 YEARS, ITEM NO. 2)

Procedure: Ask "What is that?" pointing in turn to nearby objects: shoe, watch, table, ball, chair, block, pencil, floor

Score: Four is passing.

Rationale: This item indicates a more advanced level of the child's awareness of his environment than was expected at two years, and an increasingly meaningful vocabulary. More of his verbal symbols have consistent meaning to himself and others. Although there is no reason to believe that the acquisition of new words in and of itself indicates language growth, this item indicates the child's continuing interest in communicative skills, his functioning potential, and his increasing need to identify his environment.

Reference: Gesell (1940) required children to name objects; in the Developmental Schedules (1948) pictures were substituted. Terman and Merrill used both miniature objects and pictures at this age level (1947, 1960), and Doll (1965) expected children to name ten to fifteen familiar objects.

3. SENTENCE REPETITION—INDICATES MEANINGFUL IMITATION

Procedure: Say, "Can you say 'big boy (or girl)'?" "Now say, 'I am a big boy (or girl)'." "Now say . . ."
   a. "I like to play in the water"
   b. "I have a little dog"
   c. "The dog chases the cat"
   Urge the child to respond. If necessary, say "Say it!" but do not repeat any sentence.

Score: One is passing. The child must repeat one sentence without error. Ignore faulty pronunciation.

Rationale: This item determines immediate auditory recall and memory span for meaningful material. Research indicates that it is necessary to have at least a minimal amount of rote memory skill for development of adequate linguistic skill. The child's level of mental alertness is of crucial importance in this task.
   Unlike digits, which measure memory span alone, sentences also draw upon a child's knowledge and experience in using language. Differences between digits and sentences can serve as a clue to a child's language background.

Reference: Only Gesell (1940) placed a sentence memory task at this age level, noting that at two and one-half the child can repeat a sentence of six or seven syllables in one of three trials.

4. PRONOUNCES SOUNDS CORRECTLY (I)—INDICATES CONSONANT ARTICULATION

Material: Articulation Section

Procedure: The child's attention must be focused on the examiner. Say, "We are going to play a word game now. I'll say a word first, then you say the same word after me. Listen carefully. Say, 'baby'." (practice word) If the child understands the instructions and repeats this practice word, say, "Very good!" "Now say . . ." and begin the words in Group I. However, if it is obvious that the child does not understand, repeat the instructions to him.

It is suggested that all of this Articulation Section should be given at the same time. All numbered items should be given to each child regardless of age.

The words should be scored on the child's first response. Do not repeat words.

Score: The child passes Group I of Articulation Section if *numbered* items 1 through 5 are marked plus.

The child passes a *numbered* item if all underlined sounds in the (A) word *or* both (B) and (C) words are correctly articulated. If an (A) word is repeated correctly, mark the numbered item (+) and *do not* give (B) and (C) words. Whenever an (A) word is unclear to the examiner or incorrect, give *both* the (B) and (C) words as a second trial. Success on both (B) and (C) words rates a passing score (+) on the *numbered* item. If *either* (B) or (C) words are incorrect or unclear, the *numbered* item is failed (−).

Rationale: By this age children should be able to articulate most of the vowels, the labial consonants (*p, b, m, w*), and the simpler dental consonant (*n*).

This item indicates that a child is beginning to master the lip, jaw, and tongue movements necessary to produce words. The skills required for listening to and repeating a succession of words is also within his ability.

In testing articulation, the child is asked to repeat sounds presented orally, rather than in pictorial form, in order to remove the variable of picture recognition and vocabulary knowledge measured elsewhere in this scale. Authorities in the field, such as Templin (1954), found no difference between the two methods of stimulation. Van Riper's new articulation test (in press), and Irwin (1960) in his test for cerebral palsied children, adapted the auditory method of testing for consonant production.

Reference: Authorities such as Templin (1951), Poole (1934), and
Wellman (1931) generally agree that labial sounds are
among the first to be accurately produced. Their conclu-
sions were based on a high (75%) percentile of achievement. Our experience indicates the average child of two
and one-half succeeds on this item.

3 Years (Four tests, one and one-half months each)

1. REPEATS THREE DIGITS—INDICATES ATTENTIVE VERBAL IMI-
   TATION

   Procedure: "Listen: say 4–2. Now say, 1–4–9; 9–6–1; 2–5–3." The numbers must be pronounced uniformly and distinctly at the rate of one per second.

   Score: One is passing. The child must repeat one series of three digits correctly. Ignore faulty pronunciation.

   Rationale: The child's increasing ability to listen actively, and his lengthening memory span, permit him to repeat a longer series of numbers at this stage of development.

   Reference: Digit span items were also drawn from the 1916 Binet (Terman, 1916) by Gesell (1940, 1948) and continued in the Binet in 1937 and 1960 versions.

2. USES PLURALS—INDICATES QUANTITATIVE VERBALIZATION

   Material: Picture Number 10

   Procedure: Say, "What is this?" (Point to each picture.)

   Score: Two is passing. The child should name two or more pictures of grouped objects, using the plural (shoes, blocks).

   Rationale: The use of plurals indicates that the child has acquired a systematic pattern of indicating quantity through verbal expression, and can adapt this criterion to new or novel objects in his environment. At this stage he usually adds the suffix *s* to the noun, although he may use some vowel changes such as *men*. However, the suffix *s* is usually added here also, so the child says *mens* or *mans*. By this stage, he has developed a grammatical criterion for verbal expression.

   Reference: Gesell (1940) noted that children used plurals by three years of age. The item was also in the Developmental Schedules (1948).

3. Comprehends Physical Needs—Indicates DIFFERENTIATION
OF CONCRETE EXPERIENCE (Same as 3 years, 6 months,
item no. 3 and 4 years, item no. 3)

Procedure: Say, "What do you do when you are . . ."
            a. "sleepy"
            b. "hungry"
            c. "cold"

    Score: One is passing. Sample Answers:

	Plus	*Minus*
Sleepy:	bed	get up
	lie down	ask mommy (Q)*
	rest	nothin'
	go to sleep	
Hungry:	eat	no
	candy	bed
	drink milk	ask mommy (Q)*
Cold:	coat	go out
	get warm	nothin'
	go bed	tell mommy (Q)*

Rationale: These questions consist of several conceptualizations re-
            quiring concrete and practical verbal responses. Behav-
            iors which children experience every day need to be
            verbalized in a way that is meaningful to others. Success
            on this item indicates that the child is able to differenti-
            ate between various experiences and can draw meaning-
            ful conclusions regarding cause and effect. This task
            presupposes that the child has had necessary experience
            in verbalizing solutions to practical problems and, hence,
            failure *may* suggest overprotection as well as language
            deficit. Unexpected success might be a clue to a forced
            early independence.

Reference: Similar items were used in the first Binet (Binet and
            Simon, 1908) and later by Terman and Merrill (1916)
            and Gesell (1940, 1948). Related items are on the new
            Binet (1960) and the WPPSI (1963), but not at this age
            level.

---

*Answer not improved or clarified upon questioning.

4. Gives Full Name—Indicates SELF-CONCEPT

Procedure: Say, "What is your name?" If only the first name is given, say, "(Jimmy) what?" Some urging may be necessary, but do not insist on a response.

Score: One is passing. The child should give his full name (nickname acceptable).

Rationale: This item represents a stage in a logically connected sequence of self-concept acquisition. When a child knows his own name, he begins to recognize himself as an independent individual, as well as a family member. He has differentiated himself from all others.

Reference: Knowledge of family name was noted on the first Binet (Binet and Simon, 1908). Gesell (1940) reported 85% success at age three on this item, and thus placed it at age 2 years, 6 months, maintaining this placement in the Developmental Schedules (1948). Doll (1965), on the other hand, mentioned success at 3 years, 6 months. The present placement is a compromise based on experience with the language scale.

3 Years, 6 Months (Four tests, one and one-half months each)

1. CONVERSES IN SENTENCES—INDICATES ELEMENTARY ADULT SENTENCING

Procedure: Observation. The child may be asked about his pets, family, or toys. Note whether the child uses short sentences to give information and communicate ideas.

Score: Two is passing. The child should be observed or reported to use two or more sentences conversationally. ("I have a dog. He plays with me.")

Rationale: The ability to use adult sentence structure to express ideas and information in a sensible and consistent manner is considered a measure of language ability as well as a criterion for intelligence.

This item measures the child's gain in precision of expression through his increasing use of a variety of sentences containing correct grammatical order. The item also indicates that a child cares about his speech and is judging its effectiveness, and that he trusts himself to communicate his knowledge, feelings, and ideas to others.

Reference: Gesell (1940) mentioned use of long sentences, including compound and complex structures at this age level. Terman and Merrill (1937, 1960) requested the child to tell about a picture, usually eliciting sentences but accepting individual words. Doll (1937) noted that the child can give information and convey simple ideas at this age.

2. COUNTS TO THREE—INDICATES CONSERVATION OF NUMBERS

Material: Three blocks

Procedure: Set three blocks in front of the child and say, "How many? You count them. Tell me how many is that?"

Rearrange the position of the blocks, or use three other blocks, and repeat the instructions.

Score: Two is passing. The child must count three objects correctly more than once.

Rationale: In the process of discovering "how many," the child must count the objects in sequence, and remember those already enumerated to avoid counting the same item more than once. At this age his verbal and cognitive skills have advanced to a mastery of expressing and understanding the concept of "three" when this number of objects are presented to him. He is able to conserve this numerical concept whether he is dealing with blocks, candies, toys, etc.

Reference: Doll (1965) noted that the child of 3 years, 6 months manipulated number concepts meaningfully to a number greater than two, counting to three. Gesell (1940), on the other hand, listed selecting "just two" at age three, and counting (by pointing) to three objects at age four.

3. COMPREHENDS PHYSICAL NEEDS—INDICATES DIFFERENTIATION OF CONCRETE EXPERIENCE (SAME AS 3 YEARS, ITEM NO. 3 AND 4 YEARS, ITEM NO. 3)

Procedure: Say, "What do you do when you are. . . ?"
    a. "sleepy"
    b. "hungry"
    c. "cold"

Score: Two is passing. Sample Answers:

	Plus	*Minus*
Sleepy:	bed	get up
	lie down	ask mommy (Q)*
	rest	nothin'
	go to sleep	
Hungry:	eat	no
	candy	bed
	drink milk	ask mommy (Q)
Cold:	coat	go out
	get warm	nothin'
	go bed	tell mommy (Q)

Rationale: As before, these questions consist of several conceptualizations requiring concrete and practical verbal responses, and assumes that the child has experience in verbalizing the solutions to practical problems.

---

*Answer not improved or clarified upon questioning.

Reference: Similar items were used in the first Binet (Binet and
                Simon, 1908), and later by Terman and Merrill (1916)
                and Gesell (1940, 1948). Terman and Merrill (1967) used
                the same items (but not together) on the L and M
                forms of the Binet, and related items were retained on
                the new LM Binet (1960), as well as the new WPPSI
                (1963).

4. PRONOUNCES SOUNDS CORRECTLY (II)—INDICATES CONSONANT
   ARTICULATION

Material: Articulation Section

Procedure: The child's attention must be focused on the examiner.
                Say, "We are going to play a word game now. I'll say a
                word first, then you say the same word after me. Listen
                carefully. Say, 'baby'." (practice word) If the child
                understands the instructions and repeats this practice
                word, give him reinforcement, and say "Now say . . ."
                and begin the words in Group I. However, if it is
                obvious that the child does not understand, repeat the
                instructions to him.

                It is suggested that the entire Articulation Section be
                given at the same time. All numbered items should be
                given to each child regardless of age. The words should
                be scored on the child's first response. Do not repeat
                words.

Score: The child passes Groups I and II in Articulation Section
                if *numbered* items 1 through 10 are marked plus.
                The child passes a *numbered* item if all underlined
                sounds in the (A) word *or* both (B) and (C) words are
                correctly articulated. If an (A) word is repeated cor-
                rectly, mark the numbered item (+) and *do not* give
                (B) and (C) words. Whenever an (A) word is unclear
                to the examiner or incorrect, give *both* the (B) and (C)
                words as a second trial. Success on both (B) and (C)
                words rates a pass (+) on the *numbered* item. If *either*
                (B) or (C) words is incorrect or unclear, the *numbered*
                item is failed (—).

Rationale: At this age children should have mastered the labial
                consonants and the remaining dental consonants (t) and
                (d), the gutteral consonants (k) and (g), and the voice-
                less labio-dental consonant (f).

This item indicates that a child is developing greater muscular control of his tongue when he produces words.

In testing articulation, the child is once again asked to repeat sounds presented orally, to remove the variable of picture recognition and vocabulary knowledge measured elsewhere in this scale.

Reference: Templin (1957), Poole (1934), and Wellman (1931) generally agree that the gutteral (k) and (g) and the dental (d) are among the second group of consonants to be mastered. They disagree, however, upon the developmental order in which the (t) and (f) sounds appear. Our experience indicates this item is passed at 3 years, 6 months by the average child.

4 Years (Four tests, one and one-half months each)

1. REPEATS SENTENCES—INDICATES MEANINGFUL IMITATION

Procedure: Say, "Can you say 'I am a big boy (girl)'?" "Now say. . . ."
  a. "Mary and I feed our little dog every day."
  b. "My mother and father went to the store today."
  c. "Our mother washes the dishes and sweeps the floor."
  Urge the child to respond. If necessary, say, "Say it!" but do not repeat any sentence.

Score: Two is passing. The child must repeat two sentences without any error, such as omissions, substitutions, or additions. Ignore faulty pronunciation.

Rationale: This item determines immediate auditory recall and memory span for meaningful material. Research indicates that it is necessary to have at least a minimal amount of rote memory skills for development of adequate language skills. The child's level of mental alertness is crucially important in this task. Unlike digits, which measure memory span alone, sentences also draw upon a child's knowledge and experience in using language. At this level he is expected to repeat adult sentence structure. Differences between digits and sentences can serve as a clue to a child's language background and his capacity for cognitive learning.

Reference: Terman and Merrill (1960) changed requirements for an item of this kind from two to one out of three successes, matching the Gesell (1940, 1948) requirements for repeating 12–13 syllables.

2. KNOWS OPPOSITES—INDICATES TRANSDUCTIVE THINKING (SAME AS 4 YEARS, 6 MONTHS, ITEM NO. 2)

Procedure: Say
  a. "Brother is a boy, sister is a _____."
  b. "In daytime it is light, at night it is _____."
  c. "Father is a man, mother is a _____."
  d. "The snail is slow, the rabbit is _____."
  e. "The sun shines during the day, the moon at _____."

Score: Two is passing.

	Plus	Minus
a.	girl, girlie	lady, mother
b.	dark	late, dark time
c.	woman, girl, lady	mama
d.	fast, quick, speedy	not slow, run faster
e.	night, nighttime	midnight, lights up the night

Rationale: An important factor in this item is the child's ability to comprehend relationships between words, and to produce related words which complete the thought expressed in a controlled-association task. Sufficient word availability and comprehension are also required. These factors represent transducive thinking, which is one of the structural properties necessary for future development of logical thought. It is an indication that the child's thought can be directed through particular, or controlled, channels, and is an important milestone in language production. This item measures the child's fluency in expression of sets of interrelated ideas.

Reference: The 1937 form M Binet (Terman and Merrill, 1937) used these items, which were retained in the 1960 form (Terman and Merrill, 1960).

3. COMPREHENDS PHYSICAL NEEDS—INDICATES DIFFERENTIATION OF CONCRETE EXPERIENCE (SAME AS 3 YEARS, ITEM NO. 3, AND 3 YEARS, 6 MONTHS, ITEM NO. 3)

Procedure: Say, "What do you do when you are. . . ?"
    a. "sleepy"
    b. "hungry"
    c. "cold"

Score: Three is passing. Sample Answers.

	Plus	Minus
Sleepy:	bed	get up
	lie down	ask mommy (Q)*
	rest	nothin'
	go to sleep	

---

*Answer not improved or clarified upon questioning.

Hungry:	eat	no
	candy	bed
	drink milk	ask mommy (Q)
Cold:	coat	go out
	get warm	nothin'
	go bed	tell mommy (Q)

Rationale: By this stage of development, the child should have a greater store of experiences upon which to draw, and should be able to differentiate between them to a higher degree than was expected at 3 years and at 3 years, 6 months.

Reference: Items similar to this one were used in the first Binet (Binet and Simon, 1908), and later by Terman and Merrill (1916) and Gesell (1940, 1948). Terman and Merrill (1937) used the same items separately on the L and M forms of the Binet. Related items were retained on the LM Binet (1960) and on the new WPPSI (1963).

4. Counts to Ten—Indicates NUMERICAL UNIT SERIATION

Procedure: Say, "Do you know how to count? Let's say 1–2–3. You do it: say 1–2–3 . . ." "Go on . . ."

Score: One is passing. The child must count to ten by rote without error on the first trial. Spontaneous corrections of errors are acceptable.

Rationale: This item is based on the concept that, in the development of language competence, the child must be able to understand and verbalize numerical units. The item also indicates the child's awareness of, interest in, and participation in his environment. Success indicates that the child understands numbers as a class, and is able to count serially. It also is a measure of his rote memory span.

Reference: Gesell (1940) utilized such an item, noting that children could count to ten by rote at this age, although they were unable to enumerate objects beyond the number three.

4 Years, 6 Months (Four tests, one and one-half months each)

1. REPEATS FOUR DIGITS—INDICATES ATTENTIVE VERBAL IMITATION (SAME AS 6 YEARS, ITEM NO. 1)

Procedure: Say, "Listen. Say 3–4–2. Now say: 7–2–8–1; 2–1–6–4; 6–5–9–8."

The numbers must be pronounced uniformly and distinctly at the rate of one per second. Be careful not to readminister this item if already given at age six years.

Score: One is passing. Ignore faulty pronunciation.

Rationale: The ability to listen actively is an important facet of communication. To gain competence in listening skills, and to be able to reproduce verbal symbols, the child must be able to attend to auditory stimuli and to remember them long enough to imitate them. Anderson (1953) noted that when memory span is delayed in maturing, speech development is also likely to be retarded.

Reference: Repeating four digits is listed at this age level by Gesell (1940, 1948) and on the earlier Binet (1937).

2. KNOWS OPPOSITES—INDICATES TRANSDUCIVE THINKING (SAME AS 4 YEARS, ITEM NO. 2)

Procedure: Say:

    a. "Brother is a boy, sister is a _____."
    b. "In daytime it is light, at night it is _____."
    c. "Father is a man, mother is a _____."
    d. "The snail is slow, the rabbit is _____."
    e. "The sun shines during the day, the moon at _____."

Score: Three is passing.

	Plus	*Minus*
a.	girl, girlie	lady, mother
b.	dark	late, dark time
c.	woman, girl, lady	mama
d.	fast, quick, speedy	not slow, run faster
e.	night, nighttime	midnight, lights up the night

Rationale: As with the earlier use of this item, we may see the child's growing fluency of expression, and his comprehension of interrelated ideas.

Reference: Terman and Merrill (1960) found that children could pass three of these items by the age of 4 years, 6 months, changing the items and raising slightly the order of difficulty from the 1937 version.

3. COMPREHENDS SENSES—INDICATES DIFFERENTIATION OF EX-PERIENCE (SAME AS 5 YEARS, ITEM NO. 3)

Procedure: Say, "What do you do with your eyes?"
              "What do you do with your ears?"

Score: One is passing.

	Plus	*Minus*
Eyes:	see, look, read, wink, keep shut	sleep
Ears:	listen, hear	wash, keep quiet, on head

Rationale: This item measures the child's awareness of activities performed by specific sense organs and his ability to verbalize this awareness. To succeed on this item, the child must have the capacity to understand the functions of body parts and relate them to sensory experiences.

Reference: Similar items appeared originally in the 1937 form M Binet (Terman and Merrill, 1937), and was retained in the 1960 form at this age level (Terman and Merrill, 1960).

4. COMPREHENDS REMOTE EVENTS—INDICATES ANALYSIS OF EXPE-RIENCE

Procedure: Say, "What do you do. . . ?"
              "when you have lost something"
              "before you cross the street"

Score: One is passing. Sample Answers:

	Plus	*Minus*
Lost something:	hunt, find, look	ask mommy, nothin'

Cross street: look, wait for   run
the light, wait
for mama

Rationale: These questions are based on the concept that children should be able to verbalize behaviors which are acquired and used daily. Success on this item indicates that the child is capable of solving a "life problem," and has the linguistic competence to relate the solution to another person.

This item assumes that the child has had the necessary experiences for verbalizing solutions to practical problems. The interchange between the examiner and the child concerns events and objects which are not present in the test situation; hence, the child must draw upon memory and judgment to analyze past experience. A child must develop this type of thinking for self-protection, as well as for a basis in later reasoning skills.

Reference: Similar items were taken from the original study of E. E. Lord by Gesell (1940), who further standardized the age placement.

5 Years (Four tests, one and one-half months each)

1. KNOWS COINS—INDICATES LABELING AVAILABILITY

Material: Nickel, Penny, Quarter, Dime

Procedure: Say, "What is this?" "What do we call this?" Hold up, in turn, a nickel, penny, quarter, and dime.

Score: Three is passing. The child must name three or more correctly.

Rationale: This item assumes the availability of verbal symbols as pertinent labels for everyday objects. Recognition of these societal aspects of his environment implies exposure to and interest in the world about him.

Reference: Gesell (1940) replaced a similar item from the 1916 Binet (Terman, 1916), where it was located at age six. This 5-year placement was also used on the Developmental Schedules (1948), and Doll (1965) utilized the same placement.

2. NAMES ANIMALS—INDICATES CLASS INTEGRATION AVAILABILITY (SAME AS 6 YEARS, ITEM NO. 2)

Procedure: Say, "Tell me all the animals you can think of until I tell you to stop." Continue to urge the child to respond for the full minute.

Score: Six is passing. The child must spontaneously name six animals in one minute.

Rationale: This item gives information about the presence or absence of specific verbal knowledge, and can indicate whether or not the child comes from an impoverished language background. To succeed, the child must be able to reassemble data learned in one setting and apply it in another, showing, to an extent, the amount of verbal knowledge gained through contact with adults.

   This item measures the child's fluency in producing rapidly a variety of conventional groupings, all of which involve one or more given signs or code elements.

Reference: Ilg and Ames (1964) note that at the age of five, children were able to name six animals in one minute. Animal naming is also in the new WPPSI (1963).

3. COMPREHENDS SENSES—INDICATES DIFFERENTIATION OF EX-PERIENCE (SAME AS 4 YEARS, 6 MONTHS, ITEM NO. 3)

Procedure: Say, "What do you do with your eyes?"
"What do you do with your ears?"

Score: Two is passing.

	Plus	*Minus*
Eyes:	see, look, read, wink, keep shut	sleep
Ears:	listen, hear	wash, keep quiet, on head

Rationale: This item measures the child's awareness of his sense activities and a growing ability to verbalize that awareness.

Reference: This placement is similar to the 1937 Binet form M (Terman and Merrill, 1937).

4. PRONOUNCES SOUNDS CORRECTLY (III)—INDICATES CONSONANT ARTICULATION

Material: Articulation Section

Procedure: The child's attention must be focused on the examiner. Say, "We are going to play a word game now. I'll say a word first, then you say the same word after me. Listen carefully. Say, 'baby'." (practice word) If the child understands the instructions and repeats this practice word, say, "Now say . . ." and begin the words in Group I. If it is obvious that the child does not understand the instructions, repeat them to him. All of this Articulation Section should be given at the same time, and all numbered items should be given to each child regardless of age.

The words should be scored on the child's first response. Do not repeat words.

Score: The child passes groups I, II, and III if all numbered items 1 through 15 are marked plus.

The child passes a *numbered* item if all underlined sounds in the (A) word *or* both (B) and (C) words are correctly articulated. If an (A) word is repeated correctly, mark the numbered item (+) and *do not* give (B) and (C) words. Whenever an (A) word is unclear to the examiner, or incorrect, give *both* the (B) and (C) words as a second trial. Success on both (B) and (C) words rates a passing mark (+) on the *numbered* item. If *either* (B) or (C) words is incorrect, or unclear, the *numbered* item is failed (−).

Rationale: By this stage, children will have mastered the voiced fricative (v), the sibilant blends (sh), (ch), and (dj), and the complicated tongue consonant ("l"). This mastery indicates further refinement in the developing muscular coordination and use of the speech mechanisms.

As before, the child is asked to repeat sounds presented orally rather than in pictorial form, to remove the variable of picture recognition and vocabulary knowledge measured elsewhere in this scale.

Reference: Templin (1957) places the (ch) and (sh) consonants at 4 years, 6 months, and the ("l") and (v) at six years of age; Wellman (1931) places the (ch) and (v) at five years. Our experience indicates that the average child of five years of age can pass this item.

6 Years (Four tests, three months each)

1. REPEATS FOUR DIGITS—INDICATES ATTENTIVE VERBAL IMITA-
TION (SAME AS 4 YEARS, 6 MONTHS, ITEM NO. 1)

Procedure: Say, "Listen. Say 3–4–2. Now say: 7–2–8–1; 2–1–6–4; 6–5–9–8."

The numbers must be pronounced uniformly and distinctly at the rate of one per second. Be careful not to readminister this item if already given at 4 years, 6 months.

Score: Two is passing. Ignore faulty pronunciation.

Rationale: The ability to listen actively is an important facet of communication. The child must be able to remember auditory stimuli long enough to imitate them.

Reference: Gesell (1940) noted that, at 4 years, 6 months, one series of four digits could be passed successfully, and by the age of six, two of the three series were passed. This item was also retained on the Developmental Schedules (1948).

2. NAMES ANIMALS—INDICATES CLASS INTEGRATION AVAILA-
BILITY (SAME AS 5 YEARS, ITEM NO. 2)

Procedure: Say, "Tell me all the animals you can think of until I tell you to stop." Continue to urge the child to respond for the full minute.

Score: Eight is passing. The child must spontaneously name eight animals in one minute.

Rationale: As seen in the use of this task at the earlier level, this item provides information about the presence or absence of specific verbal knowledge, and of the ability to apply data learned in one situation to another.

Reference: By age six, Ilg and Ames (1964) raised requirements for animal naming to eight in one minute. Animal naming is also in the new WPPSI (1963).

3. KNOWS MORNING VERSUS AFTERNOON—INDICATES TEMPORAL OR-
DERING DIFFERENTIATION

Procedure: Say, "Do you eat breakfast in the morning or the afternoon?"
"Do boys and girls come home from school in the
morning or in the afternoon?"
"When does afternoon start?"

Score: Three is passing. Any approximately correct response for
the third question is acceptable (after morning, twelve
o'clock, dinner time).

Rationale: A sense of temporal organization reveals the child's growing awareness of the stability and order of the world.
His temporal concepts are refined through his exploration
of his environment. At this stage of development he is
able to differentiate between places, activities, and events
by their customary temporal placement. The child is now
able to relate his knowledge of these temporal relationships to other relationships.

Reference: Gesell (1940, 1948) took a similar item from the 1916
Binet (Terman, 1916). Doll (1965) used the same concept at this age.

4. PRONOUNCES SOUNDS CORRECTLY (IV)—INDICATES CONSONANT
ARTICULATION

Material: Articulation Section

Procedure: The child's attention must be focused on the examiner.
Say, "We are going to play a word game now. I'll say a
word first, then you say the same word after me. Listen
carefully. Say, 'baby'." If the child understands the instructions and repeats this practice word, say, "Now say
. . ." and begin the words in Group I. Repeat the instructions if the child does not understand.
All numbered items should be given to each child
regardless of age.
The words should be scored on the child's first response. Do not repeat words.

Score: The child passes Groups I, II, III, and IV in Articulation Section if all numbered items 1 through 20 are
marked plus.

The child passes a *numbered* item if all underlined sounds in the (A) word *or* both (B) and (C) words are correctly articulated. If an (A) word is repeated correctly, mark the numbered item (+) and *do not* give (B) and (C) words. Whenever an (A) word is unclear to the examiner, or incorrect, give *both* the (B) and (C) words as a second trial. Success on both (B) and (C) words rates a pass (+) on the *numbered* item. If *either* (B) or (C) words is incorrect, or unclear, the *numbered* item is failed (−).

Rationale: At this stage, children should be able to articulate all consonant sounds including the sibilants (s) and (z), and the more complicated tongue movements of (r) and (th). Blends, such as (str), are also within the child's range of ability at this age.

Success on this item indicates that the child has developed all the fine muscular coordinations and the auditory discrimination skill necessary to articulate words accurately.

As before, the test is more accurate when the sounds are presented orally.

Reference: Templin (1957), Wellman (1931), and Poole (1934) disagree on the age of achievement and developmental sequence of consonant production. Our experience indicates agreement with Poole on sequential development, but we found age of achievement to be six years.

7 Years (Four tests, three months each)

1. REPEATS FIVE DIGITS—INDICATES ATTENTIVE VERBAL IMITA-
TION

Procedure: Say, "Can you say 4–7? Now say: 3–1–8–5–9; 4–8–3–7–2;
9–6–1–8–3."

The numbers must be pronounced uniformly and distinctly at the rate of one per second.

Score: One is passing. The child must repeat one of the series
in correct order.

Rationale: Success here depends on the child's ability to listen
actively, and on the kind of working relation he has with
adults. The ability to remember five digits long enough
to repeat them in correct order seems to be a good indication of the child's success in future cognitive learning
tasks. This appears to be of more predictive value with
boys than with girls. The important factor here is the
child's ability to control his own attention, memory, and
concentration span.

Reference: Digit memory has been used in all the Binet scales at
this age level (Terman and Merrill, 1937, 1960).

2. SENTENCE BUILDING—INDICATES FORMAL ADULT SENTENCING

Procedure: Say, "Listen. I'm going to tell you about cat—mouse. 'The
cat chases the mouse.' Now you make a sentence
about. . . ."
   a. "cow, bigger, pig"
   b. "boy, fell, leg"
   c. "girl, flowers, field"
If necessary, urge the child to respond by repeating
the example, saying, "Now you tell me about. . . ."

Score: The child must compose two sentences using all three
words in a related manner. Sample Answers:
   a. cow, bigger, pig: *Plus*—The pig is not bigger
                                  than the cow.
                           Minus—The cow is bigger and
                                  the pig is littler.

b. boy, fell, leg:	*Plus*—The boy fell down and hurt his leg.
	The boy has two legs and he fell.
	Minus—He fell and broke his leg.
	The boy fell with his leg.
c. girl, flowers, field:	*Plus*—The girl picks flowers in the field.
	A girl walked in the field and looked at flowers.
	Minus—The field is pretty, and a girl picks flowers.

Rationale: To solve this verbal problem, the child must understand the relationships between the classifications of words and their particular grammatical classes. For this generic relation to exist, the child must know some of the distinctions on which word-classes are based in an adult vocabulary. The child must also be able to remember the exact words given, process his inner thoughts, and supply the missing verbal elements necessary for a complete thought. Success indicates the ability to do adult sentencing.

Reference: Whipple (1914) suggested sentence building in his manual of mental tests. Later, Terman and Merrill (1937) revised an item of this kind from the more difficult 1916 format.

3. Knows Address—Indicates SELF CONCEPT

Procedure: Say, "Tell me where you live."

Score: One is passing. The child must be able to give number and street address correctly.

Rationale: This item indicates that the child is aware of his relationship to more than just his immediate home environment, and shows the degree of his increasing independence and spatial involvement. Success indicates that the child's cognitive knowledge is being incorporated into his widening environmental needs, and that he can communicate this knowledge to others. This learning is part of the basic structure for enhancing self-concept and awareness of the stability of one's world.

Reference: This kind of item is mentioned by Gesell (1948) as one
                of the skills mastered at this age.

4. PRONOUNCES SENTENCES CORRECTLY—INDICATES SENTENCE AR-
   TICULATION

Material: Articulation Section

Procedure: The examiner says, "Now we are going to say some
                sentences. Repeat just what I say, 'Ice cream and cake
                are on the table'." (practice sentence)
                   If the child understands and responds to the example,
                the examiner says, "Now say this sentence . . ." Then
                the examiner says sentence number 21. If, however, the
                child does not seem to understand what is expected of
                him, repeat the instructions and practice sentence before
                going on.
                   The words should be spoken at a rate of normal
                speech.
                   Circle words or sounds that are unclear, or incorrect,
                in the child's repetition of the test sentences.

Score: The child passes Group V if he repeats every word of
                the sentences (items 21, 22, and 23) and correctly articu-
                lates every sound therein.
                   Both correct articulation and the ability to reproduce
                the entire sentence are necessary for the child's success
                on this item. If a word is omitted, the response is incor-
                rect. However, if a word is added, the sentence is still
                counted as passed, if the child's articulation is correct.

Rationale: Since all consonants and blends should be mastered by
                the age of six, the next logical step in articulation assess-
                ment in the child's accommodation of sounds into sen-
                tence production. To be certain that these sentences are
                within the child's memory span, the length was purposely
                restricted to no more than nine syllables. Gleason (1961)
                reports that normal speakers can repeat sounds exactly,
                up to the limit imposed by their memory span. Gesell
                (1940) noted that seven to nine syllables are within the
                memory span of a three-year old; this capacity has more
                than doubled (16 to 18 syllables) by the age of six
                years. Thus, the memory factor has been deliberately

minimized here to focus instead on the articulatory fluency necessary for sentence production.

This item indicates the child's ability to repeat and to correctly articulate the more difficult consonants and blends in sentence form. The important factor is the child's ability to pronounce these sounds accurately within the framework of a sentence.

Reference: Van Riper (experimental form 1965) uses sentence repetition as part of his new test of articulation. Our research indicates the average child of seven years is able to pass this item.

74

Auditory Comprehension Checklist

NAME_____ AGE_____

BIRTHDATE_____ DATE_____

1 YEAR, 6 MONTHS
_____1. Recognizes Doll Parts (Same as 2 years, item no. 1)
_____2. Follows Directions (Same as 2 years, item no. 2)
_____3. Looks Attentively
_____4. Understands Questions

2 YEARS
_____1. Recognizes Doll Parts (Same as 18 months, item no. 1)
_____2. Follows Directions (Same as 18 months, item no. 2)
_____3. Identifies Pictures
_____4. Discriminates Pictures

2 YEARS, 6 MONTHS
_____1. Understands the Concept of the Number "One"
_____2. Compares Size (I)
_____3. Understands Use (I) (Same as 3 years, item no. 3)
_____4. Follows Simple Commands

3 YEARS
_____1. Recognizes Action
_____2. Distinguishes Prepositions (Same as 4 years, item no. 2)
_____3. Understands Use (I) (Same as 2 years, 6 months, item no. 3)
_____4. Distinguishes Parts

3 YEARS, 6 MONTHS
_____1. Recognizes Time
_____2. Compares Size (II)
_____3. Matches Sets
_____4. Groups Objects

4 YEARS
_____1. Recognizes Colors (Same as 4 years, 6 months, item no. 1)
_____2. Distinguishes Prepositions (Same as 3 years, item no. 2)
_____3. Differentiates Texture
_____4. Understands Use (II) (Same as 4 years, 6 months, item no. 4)

4 YEARS, 6 MONTHS
____1. Recognizes Colors (Same as 4 years, item no. 1)
____2. Touches Thumbs
____3. Understands the Concept of the Number "Three"
____4. Understands Use (II) (Same as 4 years, item no. 4)

5 YEARS
____1. Comprehends Right
____2. Taps Rhythm
____3. Distinguishes Weight Differences
____4. Knows Body Parts

6 YEARS
____1. Comprehends Directional Commands (I)
____2. Counts Blocks
____3. Distinguishes Animal Parts
____4. Adds numbers up to Five

7 YEARS
____1. Comprehends Directional Commands (II)
____2. Counting Taps
____3. Coin Values
____4. Adds and Subtracts Numbers up to Ten

Verbal Ability Checklist

NAME_____ AGE_____
BIRTHDATE_____ DATE_____

1 YEAR, 6 MONTHS
_____1. Uses Ten Words
_____2. Names One Picture
_____3. Asks for Simple Need
_____4. Echoes or Imitates

2 YEARS
_____1. Combines Words
_____2. Names Objects in Environment (Same as 2 years, 6 months, item no. 2)
_____3. Uses Pronouns
_____4. Refers to Self by Name

2 YEARS, 6 MONTHS
_____1. Repeats Two Digits
_____2. Names Objects in Environment (Same as 2 years, item no. 2)
_____3. Sentence Repetition
_____4. Pronounces Sounds Correctly (I)

3 YEARS
_____1. Repeats Three Digits
_____2. Uses Plurals
_____3. Comprehends Physical Needs (Same as 3 years, 6 months, item no. 3, and 4 years, item no. 3)
_____4. Gives Full Name

3 YEARS, 6 MONTHS
_____1. Converses in Sentences
_____2. Counts to Three
_____3. Comprehends Physical Needs (Same as 3 years, item no. 3, and 4 years, item no. 3)
_____4. Pronounces Sounds Correctly (II)

4 YEARS
_____1. Repeats Sentences
_____2. Knows Opposites (Same as 4 years, 6 months, item no. 2)

_____3. Comprehends Physical Needs (Same as 3 years, item no. 3, and 3 years, 6 months, item no. 3)
_____4. Counts to Ten

4 YEARS, 6 MONTHS
_____1. Repeats Four Digits (Same as 6 years, item no. 1)
_____2. Knows Opposites (Same as 4 years, item no. 2)
_____3. Comprehends Senses (Same as 5 years, item no. 3)
_____4. Comprehends Remote Events

5 YEARS
_____1. Knows Coins
_____2. Names Animals (Same as 6 years, item no. 2)
_____3. Comprehends Senses (Same as 4 years, 6 months, item no. 3)
_____4. Pronounces Sounds Correctly (III)

6 YEARS
_____1. Repeats Four Digits (Same as 4 years, 6 months, item no. 1)
_____2. Names Animals (Same as 5 years, item no. 2)
_____3. Knows Morning Versus Afternoon
_____4. Pronounces Sounds Correctly (IV)

7 YEARS
_____1. Repeats Five Digits
_____2. Sentence Building
_____3. Knows Address
_____4. Pronounces Sentences Correctly

Articulation Section

Directions: The child's attention must be focused on the examiner. "We are going to play a word game now. I'll say a word first, then you say the same word after me. Listen carefully. Say 'baby'." (practice word)

All numbered items should be given to the child, regardless of his age.

Scoring: Passes a group if all numbered items in that group are marked plus.

Passes a numbered item if all underlined sounds in the (A) word or both (B) and (C) words are correctly pronounced. If (A) word is correct, *do not* give (B) and (C) words, which provide a second trial when necessary.

GROUP I (2 yrs. 6 mos. VA)	*GROUP II* (3 yrs. 6 mos. VA)

GROUP I

____ 1. (A) <u>m</u>o<u>m</u> ____
     (B) <u>m</u>y ____
     (C) ho<u>m</u>e ____

____ 2. (A) <u>p</u>o<u>p</u> ____
     (B) <u>p</u>ie ____
     (C) ho<u>p</u> ____

____ 3. (A) <u>w</u>e ____
     (B) <u>w</u>on ____

____ 4. (A) <u>b</u>o<u>b</u> ____
     (B) <u>b</u>ee ____
     (C) we<u>b</u> ____

____ 5. (A) <u>n</u>i<u>n</u>e ____
     (B) <u>n</u>ew ____
     (C) bo<u>n</u>e ____

GROUP II

____ 6. (A) <u>d</u>i<u>d</u> ____
     (B) <u>d</u>o ____
     (C) mu<u>d</u> ____

____ 7. (A) <u>t</u>oo<u>t</u> ____
     (B) <u>t</u>o ____
     (C) ha<u>t</u> ____

____ 8. (A) <u>g</u>a<u>g</u> ____
     (B) <u>g</u>o ____
     (C) <u>d</u>og ____

____ 9. (A) <u>c</u>a<u>k</u>e ____
     (B) <u>k</u>ey ____
     (C) ba<u>k</u>e ____

____10. (A) <u>f</u>i<u>f</u>e ____
     (B) <u>f</u>un ____
     (C) pu<u>ff</u> ____

GROUP III
(5 yrs. VA)

GROUP IV
(6 yrs. VA)

____11. (A) valve ____
    (B) Vic ____
    (C) dove ____

____16. (A) zooms ____
    (B) zoo ____
    (C) buzz ____

____12. (A) little ____
    (B) like ____
    (C) ball ____

____17. (A) six ____
    (B) so ____
    (C) house ____

____13. (A) judge ____
    (B) jam ____
    (C) fudge ____

____18. (A) roar ____
    (B) rabbit ____
    (C) door ____

____14. (A) shush ____
    (B) shoe ____
    (C) push ____

____19. (A) thirteenth ____
    (B) think ____
    (C) teeth ____

____15. (A) chinch ____
    (B) chicken ____
    (C) lunch ____

____20. (A) street ____
    (B) strong ____

GROUP V (7 yrs. VA)

Directions: "Now we are going to say some sentences. Repeat just what I say. 'Ice cream and cake are on the table'." (practice sentence)

Scoring: Circle any words (or sounds) that are unclear or incorrect.

Passes Group V if all words in sentences 21, 22, and 23 are pronounced correctly.
____21. Spaceships race around the earth.
____22. Alligators never brush their teeth.
____23. A witch flies over the street.

Bibliography

Alexander, D., and J. Money, "Reading Disability and the Problem of Direction Sense," *The Reading Teacher*, 20 (1967), pp. 404-409.

Anderson, Gladys L., and J. F. Magary, "Protective Techniques and the Illinois Test of Psycholinguistics" in *School Psychological Services*, J. Magary, ed. Englewood Cliffs, N.J.: Prentice-Hall, Inc., 1967.

Arthur, Grace, *A Point Scale of Performance Tests*, Rev. Form A Manual. New York: Psychological Corporation, 1947.

Bereiter, C. S., Jean Osborn Engelman, and P. A. Reidford, "An Academically Oriented Preschool for Culturally Deprived Children," in *Preschool Education Today*, F. M. Hechinger, ed. New York: Doubleday & Company, Inc., 1965.

Binet, A., and T. Simon, "Le Développement de l'Intelligence Chez les Enfants," *L'Anée Psychologique*. 1908.

Binet, A., and T. Simon, "La Mesure du Développement de l'Intelligence Chez les Jeunes Enfants Societé Pour l'Étude, *Psychologique de l'Enfant*. Paris: 1925.

Brown, R., *Words and Things*. New York: The Free Press, 1958.

Cattell, Psyche, *Measurement of Intelligence of Infants and Young Children*. New York: The Psychological Corporation, 1947.

Cawley, J. F., "Psycholinguistic Characteristics of Preschool Children," *The Training School Bulletin*, 64 (1967), pp. 95-101.

D'Asaro, M., I. Lehrhoff, Irla Lee Zimmerman, and Margaret H. Jones, A Rating Scale for the Evaluation of Language Development in the Preschool Cerebral Palsied Child, American Academy for Cerebral Palsy, 10th Annual Session, Chicago, Illinois, 1956.

de Hirsch, Katrina, Jeannette J. Jansky, and W. S. Langford, *Predicting Reading Failure*. New York: Harper & Row, Publishers, 1966.

Doll, E. A., "Educational Management of Children with Developmental Language Disorders," *Psychology in the Schools*, 2 (1965), pp. 214-220.

Doll, E. A., "An Attainment Scale for Appraising Young Children with Expressive Handicaps," *Cerebral Palsy Journal,* 27 (1966), pp. 3-5.

Doll, E. A., *Vineland Social Maturity Scale Manual.* Educational Test Bureau, 1947.

Doll, E. A., *Preschool Attainment Record.* Minneapolis, Minn.: American Guidance Service, Inc., 1966.

DuBois, Cora, "Values: Mutable and Immutable," *AAUW Journal,* 61 (1967), pp. 12-15.

Dunn, L. M., *Peabody Picture Vocabulary Test, Manual.* Minneapolis, Minn.: American Guidance Service, Inc., 1959.

Dunn, L. M., and J. O. Smith, *Peabody Language Development Kit, Manual for Level #1.* Minneapolis, Minn.: American Guidance Service, Inc., 1965.

Ervin, S., "Imitation and Structural Change in Children's Language," in *New Directions in the Study of Language,* E. Lenneberg, ed. Cambridge, Mass.: The M.I.T. Press, 1964.

Evatt, Roberta L., Irla Lee Zimmerman, and Violette G. Steiner, "Language Assessment of Preschool Children." Paper presented at California Speech and Hearing Association Convention, Los Angeles, March 30, 1968.

Falinski, E., *Vocabulaire Orthophonique.* Institut d'Etudes Médico- Pédagogiques, Paris, Edition Jouve, 1965.

Fraser, C., U. Bellugi, and R. Brown, "Control of Grammar in Imitation, Comprehension, and Production," *Journal of Verbal Learning and Verbal Behavior,* 2 (1963), pp. 121-135.

Fulton, R. T., "Speech and Hearing Programs for the Mentally Retarded: A Model for Personnel and Facility Justification," *Mental Retardation,* 5 (1967), pp. 27-33.

Gesell, A., *Developmental Schedules.* New York: The Psychological Corporation, 1956.

Gesell, A., *The First Five Years of Life.* New York: Harper & Row, Publishers, 1940.

Gesell, A. L., and Catherine S. Amatruda, *Developmental Diagnosis.* New York: Harper & Row, Publishers, 1948.

Glasser, Alan J., and Irla Lee Zimmerman, *Clinical Interpretation of the WISC.* New York: Grune & Stratton, Inc., 1967.

Gleason, H. A., *An Introduction to Descriptive Linguistics.* New York: Holt, Rinehart & Winston, Inc., 1961.

Haeussermann, Else, *Developmental Potential of Preschool Children.* New York: Grune & Stratton, Inc., 1958.

Hodges, W. L., and H. H. Spicker, "The Effects of Preschool Experiences on Culturally Deprived Children," in *The Young Child, Review of Research,* W.W. Hartup and Nancy L. Smothergill, eds. Washington, D.C.: National Association for the Education of Young Children, 1967, pp. 262-289.

Holbrook, S. M. A., "A Psychological Study of a Group of Three Year Old Children." Master's thesis, Yale University, 1922.

Ilg, Frances L., and Louise B. Ames, *School Readiness.* New York: Harper & Row, Publishers, 1964.

Irwin, O. C., "Language and Communication" in *Handbook of Research in Child Development,* P. H. Mussen, ed. New York: John Wiley & Sons, Inc., 1960.

John, Vera P., and L. S. Goldstein, "The Social Context of Language Acquisition," *Merrill Palmer Quarterly,* 10 (1964), pp. 265-275.

Jones, Katherine L. S., "The Language Development of Head Start Children." Master's thesis, University of Arkansas, 1966.

Kinsler, Elizabeth, "Language Development in the Normal Child," *The Voice,* 16 (1966), pp. 8-15.

Kirk, S. A., and J. J. McCarthy, *The Illinois Test of Psycholinguistic Abilities: An Approach to Differential Diagnosis.* American Journal of Mental Deficiency, 66 (1961), pp. 399-412.

Kuhlman, F. A., *A Handbook of Mental Tests, A Further Revision of Binet Simon Tests of Mental Development.* Baltimore, Md.: Warwick and York, 1922; Minneapolis, Minn.: Educational Test Bureau, 1939.

Lovell, K., and E. M. Dixon, "The Growth of the Control of Grammar in Imitation, Comprehension, and Production," *Journal of Child Psychology and Psychiatry,* 8 (1967), pp. 31-39.

McCarthy, Dorothy A., *The Language Development of the Preschool Child.* Minneapolis, Minn.: University of Minnesota Press, 1930.

Mecham, M. J., *Verbal Language Development Scale, Manual.* Beverly Hills, Calif.: Western Psychological Services, 1958.

Metraux, R. W., "Speech Profiles of the Preschool Child 18 to 54 Months," *Journal of Speech and Hearing Disorders,* 15 (1950), pp. 137-153.

Muntz, L. A., *A Study of Individual Differences in Two Year Old Children.* Master's thesis, Yale University, 1921.

Myklebust, H. R., *Development and Disorders of Written Language.* New York: Grune & Stratton, Inc., 1965.

Piaget, J., *The Origins of Intelligence in Children.* New York: W. W. Norton & Company, Inc., 1963.

84

Piaget, J., *The Child's Conception of Number*. New York: W. W. Norton & Company, Inc., 1965.

Poole, I., "General Development of Articulation of Consonant Sounds," *Elementary English Review* (1934), pp. 154-161.

Powers, Margaret H., "Functional Disorders of Articulation, Symptomatology, and Etiology," in *Handbook of Speech Pathology*, L. E. Travis, ed. New York: Appleton-Century-Crofts, 1957.

Robinson, H. B., and Nancy M. Robinson, *The Mentally Retarded Child*. New York: McGraw-Hill Book Company, 1965.

Sharp, Florence, "Speech Deficiency and Retardation," *The Voice*, 14 (1965), pp. 3-11.

Silver, A. A., M. S. Pfeiffer, and Rosa A. Hagin, "The Therapeutic Nursery as an Aid in the Diagnosis of Delayed Language Development," *American Journal of Orthopsychiatry*, 37 (1967), pp. 963-970.

Simon, C. T., "Development of Speech," in *Handbook of Speech Pathology*, L. E. Travis, ed. New York: Appleton-Century-Crofts, 1957.

Smith, F. A., and G. A. Miller, *The Genesis of Language*. Cambridge, Mass.: The M.I.T. Press, 1966.

Springer, Doris, "Development in Young Children of an Understanding of Time and the Clock," *Journal of Genetic Psychology*, 80 (1952), pp. 83-96.

Stearns, K. E., "Experimental Group Language Development for Psycho-Socially Deprived Preschool Children." Master's thesis, Indiana University, 1966.

Steiner, Violette G., Irla Lee Zimmerman, and Roberta L. Evatt, "Differential Diagnosis of Preschool Language Development," *American Psychologist*, 23 (1968), p. 615.

Stutsman, Rachel, *Mental Measurement of Preschool Children, with a Guide for the Administration of the Merrill-Palmer Scale of Mental Tests*. Chicago: World Book Encyclopedia, Inc., 1931.

Taylor, Edith M., *Psychological Appraisal of Children with Cerebral Defects*. Cambridge, Mass.: Harvard University Press, 1961.

Templin, Mildred C., *Certain Language Skills in Children*. Minneapolis, Minn.: University of Minnesota Press, 1957.

Templin, Mildred C., "Research on Articulation Development," in *The Young Child: Reviews of Research*. W. W. Hartup and Nancy L. Smothergill, eds. Washington, D.C.: National Association for the Education of Young Children, 1967.

Templin, Mildred, and F. Darley, *The Templin-Darley Tests of Articulation Manual and Discussion.* Washington, D.C.: Bureau of Educational Research, 1960.

Terman, L. M., *The Measurement of Intelligence.* New York: Houghton Mifflin Company, 1916.

Terman, L. M., and Maud A. Merrill, *Stanford Binet Intelligence Scale, Manual for Third Revision, Form L-M.* Boston: Houghton Mifflin Company, 1960.

Terman, L. M., and Maud Merrill, *Measuring Intelligence.* Boston: Houghton Mifflin Company, 1937.

Todd, Vivian E., and Helen Hefferman, *The Years Before School: Guiding Preschool Children.* New York: The Macmillan Company, 1964.

Valett, R. E., *Profile for Stanford Binet.* Palo Alto, Calif.: Consulting Psychologists Press, 1966.

Valett, R. E., *Developmental Survey of Basic Learning Abilities.* Palo Alto, Calif.: Consulting Psychologists Press, 1966.

Van Riper, C., *Predictive Screening Test of Articulation.* Kalamazoo, Michigan: Western Michigan University, 1965, 2nd Experimental Form (unpublished).

Van Riper, C., *Speech Correction: Principles and Methods* (Fourth Edition). Englewood Cliffs, N.J.: Prentice-Hall, Inc., 1954.

Wechsler, D., *WPPSI Manual.* New York: The Psychological Corporation, 1963.

Wellman, Beth L., Ida M. Case, Ida G. Mengert, and Dorothy E. Bradbury, "Speech Sounds of Young Children," *University of Iowa Studies in Child Welfare,* 2 (1931).

Whipple, C. M., *Manual of Mental and Physical Tests.* New York: Warwick and York, 1914.

Zimmerman, Irla Lee, "Intelligence Testing," in *School Psychological Services,* J. F. Magary, ed. Englewood Cliffs, N.J.: Prentice-Hall, Inc., 1967.

Zimmerman, Irla Lee, Violette G. Steiner, and Roberta L. Evatt, "A Speech Scale for Head Start Children: Preliminary Report." Paper presented at California State Psychological Association Convention, San Diego, January 27, 1967.

Zimmerman, Irla Lee, Violette G. Steiner, and Roberta L. Evatt, "Utilizing Educational Psycholinguistics in Early Childhood," (in preparation).

Zimmerman, Irla Lee, Violette G. Steiner, and Roberta L. Evatt, "Verbal Imitation Skills of American, English, and French Preschool Children," (in preparation).